MW00770776

A THEOLOGY IN OUTLINE

A THEOLOGY IN OUTLINE
Can These Bones Live?

Robert W. Jenson

Transcribed, edited, and introduced
by **Adam Eitel**

OXFORD
UNIVERSITY PRESS

Oxford University Press is a department of the University of Oxford. It furthers
the University's objective of excellence in research, scholarship, and education
by publishing worldwide.Oxford is a registered trade mark of Oxford University
Press in the UK and certain other countries.

Published in the United States of America by Oxford University Press
198 Madison Avenue, New York, NY 10016, United States of America.

© Oxford University Press 2016

All rights reserved. No part of this publication may be reproduced, stored in
a retrieval system, or transmitted, in any form or by any means, without the
prior permission in writing of Oxford University Press, or as expressly permitted
by law, by license, or under terms agreed with the appropriate reproduction
rights organization. Inquiries concerning reproduction outside the scope of the
above should be sent to the Rights Department, Oxford University Press, at the
address above.

You must not circulate this work in any other form
and you must impose this same condition on any acquirer.

Library of Congress Cataloging-in-Publication Data
Names: Jenson, Robert W.
Title: A theology in outline : can these bones live? / Robert W. Jenson ;
transcribed, edited, and introduced by Adam Eitel.
Description: New York : Oxford University Press, 2016. | Includes
bibliographical references.
Identifiers: LCCN 2015035941 | ISBN 978–0–19–021459–3 (cloth : alk. paper)
Subjects: LCSH: Theology, Doctrinal.
Classification: LCC BT80 .J46 2016 | DDC 230—dc23 LC record available at
http://lccn.loc.gov/2015035941

10
Printed by Sheridan, USA

CONTENTS

PREFACE

Robert W. Jenson

Adam Eitel's Introduction leaves aside two things he could not do and that I must do now. One is to thank him. The idea for this book was his, the impetus was his, and he did almost all the labor. I am very grateful. Indeed I am honored that someone with such theological talent should have devoted so much of his time and his energy to my work.

The second thing I must do is to reflect on what I was trying to do in the lectures on which this book is based. The title of the book—*A Theology in Outline*—does not quite capture what I was trying to give the undergraduates who attended those lectures. I think the best word for what I wanted to give them is "taste": I wanted them to *taste* a bit of Christian theology, that unaccustomed food, in hopes that they might find it savory.

A THEOLOGY IN OUTLINE

Introduction

Adam Eitel

It is good whenever possible to skip introductions, and to at least many readers Robert Jenson needs none. Beginning in 1961, and spanning over half a century, Jenson's writings bridge disciplines and discourses that we moderns tend to keep separate: biblical studies, ethics, philosophy, theology, ecumenism, and interreligious dialogue. The list is not exhaustive. I do not need to expound here on the very large influence of Jenson's efforts. But we cannot altogether skip an introduction, for the nature of the present volume cannot be well understood apart from its origins.

A Theology in Outline began with an undergraduate course taught by Jenson at Princeton University in the spring of 2008. As a beneficiary of the university's Center for the Study of Religion, and thanks in large part to Jeffrey Stout, in the early 2000s the Department of Religion was able to invite several prominent theologians to teach courses in Christianity. Jenson's course—"'Can These Bones Live?' An Introduction to Christian Theology"—introduced students to a standard sequence of topics in Christian theology: God, Trinity, creation, humanity, sin, salvation, and church. The course's *leitmotiv* and organizing principle was somewhat less traditional. As its title suggests, the course framed the whole of Christian theology as a response to the question posed to the prophet Ezekiel: "Son of man, can these bones live?" (Ezekiel 37:3). If Ezekiel's valley of bones is a metaphor, to what does it refer? Jenson's answer was twofold. To ask whether these bones can live is to ask, first, whether the story that God lives with his people can continue. Then, too, one can ask: is the Christian faith itself a pile of dead and dried up bones? Is Christian theology dead?

From first to last the course proceeded under the impelling pressure of these questions.

More than fifty students registered for the course, but many more than that attended. The room was often filled to capacity because of auditors, who included seminarians, professors, visiting scholars, and local clergy. Mondays and Wednesdays, this motley crew gathered to hear Jenson speak. Officially registered students also attended weekly discussion groups led by Jenson or a department lecturer—Matthew Rose or myself. Known locally as "precepts" and in other contexts as "tutorials," these small, seminar-style sessions focused on the course readings. We read nearly all of Genesis, the Gospel of Mark, large portions of Acts and the epistles, as well as representative selections from Exodus, Job, and the prophets—not least Ezekiel. Athanasius's *On the Incarnation*, Augustine's *Confessions*, and Hildegard of Bingen's *Scivias*, I–VI, as well as Luther's *On Christian Liberty* and Jonathan Edwards's *The Nature of True Virtue* were also read in full. The last few weeks of the course were devoted to grappling with Dietrich Bonhoeffer's *Letters and Papers from Prison* and Hans Urs von Balthasar's *Mysterium Paschale*. Needless to say this was no typical introduction to theology.

When lecturing, Jenson always came with something specific to say, and on most days he would go on at length. Yet he did not read from a manuscript; he brought notes from which he spoke more or less ex tempore. He moreover encouraged and at times nearly *insisted* on interjections: questions, protestations, provocations, and requests for clarity. That is to say, even his lectures were not so much lectures as *conversations*. In this respect they were lived enactments of what Jenson takes theology to be: a long, inextricably interpersonal series of deliberations on the gospel.

A Theology in Outline is not a summary of Jenson's renowned *Systematic Theology*. It is an exemplary instance of his teaching. It is an *outline*, then, in the precise sense that it is an itinerary for doing theology. Several editorial stages have intervened between the original lectures and the chapters that follow. The earliest manuscript consisted in a transcription of audio recordings of the lectures, which Jenson and I then divided into chapters for publication. The text presented here is lightly polished verbatim. Nothing new has been added, though in some instances material has been reordered. Several cuts were made as well. The most conspicuous among them are Jenson's dialogical exchanges with students and his expositions of the assigned readings. Despite these omissions I think readers will find that the atmosphere of Jenson's classroom remains.

Chapter 1—"What Is Theology?"—insists that the character of Christian theology is immanently specific to the nature of the church, the community generated around the news that the God of Israel has raised Jesus of Nazareth from the dead. The second and third chapters elaborate the content of this gospel. Chapter 2, "Israel," centers on Israel's memory of its own story as told by the Old Testament: beginning with the story of Abraham and, again, with Moses, the God of Israel reveals himself to be a God who *speaks*. As Jenson understands it, Israel's relationship with this talkative God culminates in the Lord's question to Ezekiel: "can these bones live?" Has death won? Chapter 3, "Jesus and Resurrection," portrays the empty tomb as the Lord's own answer to this question. The fourth chapter—"The Triune God"—specifies what Jenson has called the primary dramatis personae of Jesus's resurrection. This sets the stage for Chapter 5, "Creation." God, says Jenson, calls the world into being in the same way he calls into being Israel and the church. God speaks. Chapter 6, "The Image of God," specifies the nature of human beings—divine image bearers—whom God calls to participate in this Triune discourse. Jenson argues that the biblical notion of the image in fact differs from the standard portrayals: to be made in God's own image is to be a creature with whom God can strike up a *conversation*. Or again, a human being is distinguished from other animals insofar as he or she is a *praying animal*.

If the first six chapters insist that God creates all things by divine speech, the seventh chapter, "Sin and Salvation," makes explicit the inextricably *moral* content of that speech. Human beings are created for living faithfully and lovingly in community with God and one another; sin is whatever breaks up this community. What then is salvation? Jenson's answer hails from Luther's *On Christian Liberty*. With the eighth chapter, "Church," the discourse turns toward the community gathered around the news of Christ's resurrection. The New Testament insists that the church is Christ's own body. From this Jenson concludes that the church is nothing less than Christ's availability to the world. At last, the ninth and final chapter—"Can These Bones Live?"—revisits some doubts enunciated in Chapter 1: can the church and its theology survive the withering critique of modern nihilism? I leave it to readers to discover for themselves how Jenson answers this question.

My thanks go to Matthew Bruce and Christopher Dickson, who read portions of this manuscript during its earliest stages. Some of the transcriptions were supported by a grant from the J. William Fulbright Program. The rest would not have been finished without the help of G. B. McClanahan; my thanks go to him as well. I would also like to recognize Keith Johnson, who assembled the bibliography that appears at the end of this volume. Finally, Cynthia Read deserves special thanks for seeing this project through. The book is of course Jenson's, not mine, but I wish to dedicate what work I have put into it to him—a great theologian, teacher, and friend.

1 | What Is Theology?

What is theology? The word "theology" is derived from the Greek *theologia,* which, when literally translated, means something like "reasoned talk about God." In this very general sense, theology is going on all over the place. Jews, Christians, Muslims, most varieties of Hindus, and many others besides talk about God or the gods—and for the most part they try to be reasonable in the process. But the analogies between what each of these communities calls "theology" are fairly thin. Thus the analogies between what Jews or Christians mean by "the LORD God" and what the Advaita Hindu means by "the Absolute" are thin. It is a stretch to say they are all doing same thing when doing theology because it is a stretch to say they are all talking about the same thing. Theology, insofar as it is a discourse and discipline, turns out to be immanently specific.

Yet, it is not just *what* a community says about God, the gods, the Absolute, but also the very procedures, grammar, and logical rules of its discourse that distinguish its theology from the theology of other religious communities. What a community is up to when it is doing theology depends on what sort of community it is. Every community, then, that isn't altogether dead (and one of the questions we must ask is whether the Christian community is not altogether dead) harbors a conversation about its own purpose. This goes for two members of the Elks Club sitting at a bar trying to decide what they should do at the next social meeting. It applies, too, to what the United States Supreme Court does when it tries to interpret the US Constitution in the twenty-first century. In the case of the Christian community, we Westerners are likely to call this conversation "Christian theology." This is what I intend to introduce you to now.

Obviously, then, the first thing I have to do is to say what sort of community the Christian church is. Is it more like the Elks Club or a corporation? Like a family or like a nation? What is it? It must be admitted right from the start that different communions propose different descriptions of what kind of community the Christian church is—at least as their first and preferred description. The more catholic varieties of Christianity are likely to insist that the church is a sacramental community. Where the church is real, they will say, is where people are gathered around the bread and the wine of the Lord's Supper, the water of baptism, and even minor sacraments such as the sign of the cross. The Baptists, on the other hand, will tell you that the church is a community of prayer, praise, and proclamation. Those are different answers. There is, however, a kind of minimalist definition that I think both can agree on—even if it is not their preferred description.

All agree that the church is the community of a *message*. What the church lives for and what holds it together is not an ethic. Neither the Golden Rule nor the Sermon on the Mount is what the church is all about in the first instance. Nor does the church live for a political agenda from the left or from the right. Still less is the church a celebratory praxis. What the church lives for and what holds it together is rather a piece of alleged *news*—a *message* that is thought to be so important that it absolutely must be passed on. More or less all branches of the Christian church and branches of the churches' theology will say something like this. Or anyway, that is the case where the church is even slightly faithful to itself.

Now then—what about this message? The specifically Christian community began when certain first-century Jews came to believe through events they experienced that Jesus of Nazareth—the rabbi, prophet, and healer, whose disciples they had been, and who had been executed as a threat to the religious and political establishment—had been raised from the dead by the God of Israel. Contrary to what might have been expected, this counterintuitive, implausible piece of news was not ignored. Quite the contrary. It has been circulated through the whole of subsequent history by being passed from one person to another for nearly two thousand years. The church has often called this piece of news "the gospel." Then, too, it has considered this piece of alleged news, this gospel, to be a matter of life and death to anyone and everyone who hears it. It obviously takes a plurality of people for this message to be carried on: *A* tells *B* and, if *B* believes (and in the majority of cases *B* will not), then *B* tells *C*, and so on. According to the minimal definition I am searching for here, the community thus created is the church.

If the church is the community of a message, what then is Christian theology? It is the *thinking* involved in making that move from *B* to *C*, from hearing the gospel to speaking it. The gospel differs from many sorts of news in this regard. If I tell you, "the cat is on the mat" and you have to tell someone else this, you can just parrot what you heard from me. The switch from hearing to speaking the gospel, by contrast, takes some thinking. Indeed, it takes a lot of thinking. Why? Because questions press themselves on all sides.

First this. What in the world could it mean that someone has been *raised* from the dead? Resurrections, after all, do not happen every day. It is unclear whether such a thing is possible. Nor is it clear what such an event would look like. When you say, "Jesus is raised from the dead," what are you saying happened to him? Did he have a near-death experience from which he recovered? Was he resuscitated? Did his corpse somehow disappear? The Gospel stories about the resurrection describe people coming to the tomb and finding it empty. What if they found a corpse there? Would that have proven that Jesus was not raised from the dead? There is a long running argument on that point within all branches of Christian theology. (The second greatest theologian of the twentieth century, Rudolf Bultmann, thought there must have been a corpse in the tomb. But that, Bultmann insisted, did not mean that Jesus was not raised from the dead.) If someone claimed to have seen a person walking about after being killed (which is what the disciples claimed), even if you believed it—how would you know precisely *what* you had seen? You can see why the Gospels include the story about doubting Thomas.

In the second place, it is unclear how to understand the claim that it was the God of *Israel* who raised Jesus from the dead. This implicates a whole other community besides the church into the message that the church has to carry on. It turns out that you cannot well understand what you must say in order to be saying the gospel unless you know a *whole lot* about the Jews. "Who is this God of Israel?" That was the question Moses asked upon being accosted by a supernatural phenomenon on Mount Horeb.

Its answer took a long time to work out. So who is this God of Israel? How is he different from other candidate gods? Is "he," the pronoun I have been using, the right pronoun?

Then, third, it is not even obvious what it means to be dead. When we say, "the God of Israel has raised the servant Jesus from the dead," what do we mean by "dead"? What happens to us when we die? Is there a piece of us that keeps going? A so-called immortal soul? Or is death just entering into nothingness? And if so, what would that be like? Let me give you an experiment you can work on (I once wrote the first half of a book on this point): try to imagine your own death. You will find you cannot do it because you will simply be imagining yourself experiencing something else: it might be blackness, coldness, nothingness, a void, heaven, hell, and so on—but it in each case it will be *something*. It follows that you are not in fact imagining your death. You are simply imagining yourself living a different mode of life. So what does it mean to say that someone is dead?

A fourth and most essential questions is, "Who is this Jesus?" After all, the claim that "God has raised Josef Stalin from the dead" would not be good news to a very large number of people. Even the current dictator of Russia would be dismayed, for he would lose his job. So in order to make that move from hearing the gospel to speaking it, you need to know who Jesus is. And here again there are a variety of suppositions around. Most of them are pretty balmy. The ones that claim to be earth-shaking and ground-breaking are bologna.

Finally, what would it mean to actually live on the supposition that Jesus indeed lives? What in university curricula is labeled "ethics" is, in Christian theology, not something distinct from theology. Theology, you see, is ethics too. So there is a sizable intellectual responsibility involved in being at point *B*. For if I have heard the gospel and if I believe it, I am now obliged to not only speak it but to live as if it is true. But on account of these questions and many others it is not at all clear what I am to say or do.

Each of these questions is in some sense implied by the sub-title of these lectures, "Can These Bones Live?" During the first part of the sixth century BC, Babylon was busy subjugating the little kingdoms of the Fertile Crescent or, failing that, destroying them. With the Jewish state, Babylon first tried the former, taking hostages of the Jewish leadership to Babylon in 597. Among them was the priest Ezekiel, who became a prophet. As Babylon moved on toward the total destruction of Jerusalem, Ezekiel had a prophetic vision, recorded in chapter 37 of his book, of the Jewish nation as a people of dried out bones. The Lord showed him a valley full of bones so well and truly dead that they no longer made skeletons. And the Lord asked him a question, "Son of a Man, what do you think? Can these bones live again?" There is a way in which the whole story of Israel—everything that had happened to it from the call of Abraham—had led up to that question. The people of God were dead. The nation was finished. And the question was, "can death be reversed?" And that is indeed *the* question. Does death win? Has it already won? Is death not the champion of our own time? Is not the killing of six million Jews and a few less million Cambodians and the continuing slaughter that is going on right now—does that not more or less prove that death has indeed won?

The church and its thinking—its theology—begins with that little group of Jews who became convinced that Jesus's resurrection was God's own answer to the question the Lord posed to Ezekiel. They declared that the dead bones of God's people, Israel, and the dead bones of humanity in general can indeed live again. Jesus's first disciples thought they should pass on this news. Death does not win, they said. Indeed they sang it: "Oh death, where is thy sting? Oh grave, where is thy victory?" So that is the one side of the question from Ezekiel that I put as the sub-title of these lectures. The other side of the question is this: can the church and its theology live? Is the gospel—the church's message that death does not win because it does not win with Jesus—is that message still tenable? Is Christian theology itself a pile of dried up bones? Does it still make sense to say that someone has risen from the dead? And if it does, did it in fact happen? And even if a first-century Galilean rabbi did rise from the dead, so what? What has that got to do with me? Why should the Jews and their God and this Jewish rabbi have any special role in my life or in yours? And can we really know anything, rightly or wrongly, about who this Jesus of Nazareth is? Can we give answers to these questions that are actually intelligible to twenty-first-century denizens of the modern West? Well, can these bones live?

We cannot take up this last set of questions without answering the other set first. To do so we are going to proceed through a more or less standard list of topics in a more or less traditional order: we shall speak, for example, of God, creation, human beings, sin, salvation, and the church. But to do so we need to start with a surprisingly somewhat less standard topic—namely, Jesus of Nazareth. Yet, we cannot understand Jesus without first understanding the God of Israel. This brings us to the Old Testament, which of course existed long before the church.

2 | Israel

The Old Testament was there before the church was. So the question was never about whether this church—this *ecclesia*, this gathering around this message—could accept the Old Testament. The question was rather whether the Old Testament could accept the church. Could Jesus be plausibly seen as fulfilling the Old Testament? Could he be plausibly seen as an answer to the Lord's question to Ezekiel?

The Old Testament tells Israel's story as Israel remembered it. Now, this point requires some comment. The historical memory of a people or of an individual is built up and reshaped as time goes by. Previously unnoticed events register in light of new events, old events are seen differently in light of new events, and this goes on and on as long as a people or an individual lives. Israel's historical memory of itself was built up, reshaped, and handed on this way for almost two thousand years.

So long as a people is alive, there will be an exchange between how it remembers its history at any given time and its needs, concerns, and goings-on in the present. There is thus usually a difference between a people's own living memory of its history and the accounts constructed by historians—critical scholars who do not share the living history of the people in question. At a few points I will look at the difference between the biblical documentation of how Israel remembered its past and the rather duller accounts sometimes constructed by critical scholars. But for the most part I am going to let Israel tell its own story in its own way. And that means we will be doing theology right from the start. For the way that Israel remembered its history was as a history begun, carried on, and indeed shared by its God.

In Israel's memory and so in the Old Testament, the story had two beginnings. Both are calls by God to an individual—namely, Abraham and Moses. We read in Genesis 12:1–3, "so the LORD said to Abram . . ." Notice that his name is missing a syllable. Abram is his pagan name; he is not yet called. To this man, the Lord said, "I will make of you a great nation, and in you all the families of the earth shall be blessed." In a way, the whole story of Israel is already contained in those few sentences. We are told nothing at all about why God called Abram and not some-one else. We are simply told that there was once a tribesman in present-day northern Iraq. And then *whoosh*—the Lord spoke to him. Why Abram? No one knows. All we can say is that if the Lord wanted to be represented in history, it had to start with someone and at some time. That is all we discover.

Astonishingly, Abram did what he was told. And it turned out that this brought him a lifetime of traveling hither and yon. A big part of the Old Testament is devoted to his adventures as he migrated along the borders of present-day Lebanon, Jordan, and Palestine. Much else is devoted to the subsequent adven-tures of his son Isaac, Isaac's son Jacob, and Jacob's twelve sons from whom the famous tribes of Israel are named. From the sto-ries that the Old Testament tells, ethnologists would classify the people of Abraham, Isaac, and Jacob as a semi-nomadic group living off their herds, meaning that they will settle down on the edges of properly agricultural civilizations and stay as long as the climate and politics are convenient. But the book of Genesis is not really part of an ethnographical description. For it starts right off with God. So right from the beginning we have to look at what the story says about God and his relationship to Abram. There are several things to be noted.

First, God *talks* to Abram. We are not here told how that works. Did Abram hear things in the middle of the night? Did someone pop up in the night and say, "I am God and this is what I have to say?" We do not know. But the analogy of subsequent stories about Abraham suggests that we can at least say this much: the notion that God talks to Abraham is not intended metaphorically. Those who are pious often say, "God said to me . . ." and mean it as a metaphor; it means, "I felt that way strongly and am inclined to in some way attribute those feelings to the Holy Spirit." That is just fine. But it is not what is intended here. Rather, somehow or other an actual conversation takes place between God and Abram. And that will be characteristic of the relationship between God and the people of Israel throughout their entire history together. The God of Israel is a talkative one. There is a *terrible* hymn that talks about the silence of eternity. It cannot be right, for the Jewish God cannot keep his mouth shut! He is talkative! And he moreover expects to be answered!

The second thing the passage suggests is that this is a God who has a people with whom he speaks. That indeed is the whole point of Abraham who, once he was called, was given a new name—it means "the father of many peoples." God gets started with creating a particular people who will be his people and whom he expects to hear him. Moreover, by this conversation between God and Israel, the Lord seeks to gain access to all the families of the earth. It is as if Israel were one huge prophet; the blessing of listening to God is not given to Israel for Israel's own sake but for the sake of opening up a *conversation* between the human race and this lively, talkative God. People who saw Abraham as their primal ancestor handed on the great stories about Abraham not only because they were great (and yes, strange) stories. They handed them on because they conceived of God as someone about whom stories can be told.

You must understand how religiously atypical this notion of God truly is. It is the great maxim of pre-Jewish, pre-Christian religion (and now, of post-Christian religion) that though it is nice to tell stories about God or the gods, such stories are not to be taken with final seriousness. The Greeks after all knew perfectly well that Zeus did not have a complaining wife. There was just something *about* Zeus that could be illustrated with such stories. Not so with the God of Israel! In this case, there is an actual, particular people, about whom stories can be told; and their God is so involved with this people—so taken up in conversation with them—that their stories are his stories too. Now that may be right or wrong. But it is unique. This is a religion wherein people tell stories about themselves that are also simultaneously about God.

Abraham's descendants saw God this way because they believed he had in fact called Abraham and had gone adventuring with him. Now, that is of course a circle. They saw God this way because they believed that he called Abraham and went adventuring out with him, and they talked about Abraham that way because they see God that way. That is a circle, but not a vicious one. It is called a hermeneutical circle, and it develops in every serious intellectual enterprise.

Now, if the God depicted in the Old Testament—the God who starts up a history with a particular tribal chief—is the God that actually is, then we have already come to a major theological claim. This God does not ride serenely above the historical reality of the temporal world as does the god imagined by Western modernity. Modernity's particular religion, often called Deism, believes in God but thinks that God must be immune to and uninvolved with the vicissitudes, happenings, and contingent chances that make up our history and time. The God depicted in the Old Testament does not ride serenely above the happenings of the temporal world. Israel's God lives the history of this world together with us. And that means he has to live by and with the particularities and singularities of history. He has to enter history the same way that anyone enters history: by taking a particular place and doing particular things. And he does that the way anyone does: by identifying himself with a particular cause or people or movement—in fact, Israel.

Israel may of course have been wrong about its historical relationship to God, in which case there is no reason to suppose that God is involved in our history at all. For as it happens, Judaism and Christianity are the two great faiths that see God this way. Now in a university course I am not supposed to try to *convince* you that God actually did involve himself in humanity by involving himself with the Jewish people and calling Abraham. But I can remark that it is the only proposal on the table for a God present to us not merely above our history but also from inside of it. Of course, we may ask if there really was an Abraham and his tribe. The best we can say, I think, is that the descriptions in Genesis of their way of life and their adventures fit with what we otherwise know of the conditions and migrations in that early part of the second millennium. Personally, I am always more inclined to trust in an ancient people's own account of themselves than what modern critical scholars may dream up as replacements for them.

And now we turn to Israel's other beginning: Moses and the Exodus. The biblical story of the wanderings of Abraham, Isaac, and Jacob breaks off with the Israelites fleeing south through a terrible drought. There was no grazing for their herds so they fled south looking for water and pasture until they were settled in Egypt by a friendly Pharaoh. There they stayed for some centuries, probably from around 1700 to sometime after 1300 BC. We are told absolutely nothing about what happened then other than that they multiplied. Exodus picks up Israel's story as though Israel is just starting from scratch. And in a way it is. We find the Israelites as an oppressed minority in Egypt who moreover have apparently forgotten all about the God of Abraham. The book of Ezekiel suggests that they were worshiping the Egyptians' gods.

Israel's story of the Exodus—of this new beginning—begins when Moses, an Israelite with an Egyptian name, kills an Egyptian whom he finds beating another Israelite. Moses flees to the Sinai Peninsula, where he settles among the locals, marries, and goes to work for his father-in-law. One day he leads a flock to pasture at Mount Sinai or Horeb. There, God speaks to him just as God spoke to Abraham. The Lord tells Moses that he has now heard the groans of the Israelites and has decided to do something about it. He will bring them out of Egypt, and Moses is to take care of that.

The historical character of God's relationship to Israel appears here in particularly blatant and troubling fashion: during the time of their oppression, God does not seem to have thought about Israel. It is not until God hears their groans that the promises made to Abraham get picked back up. "Go tell the people," God says, "that I have sent you to lead them from Egypt, to lead you to the place that Abraham started off for. And go tell Pharaoh to let them go."

Moses objects that no one will pay any attention to him. His objection is followed by a profound question: "Who are you? Who exactly is it that I am talking with?" Notice that he has to ask! It is as though Israel were starting over again! "The people who I am going to now lead have a right to know who this god is," says Moses. God answers with an evasion: "I will be who I will be." Moses keeps on pressing, and finally he gets a *Name*.

I will not speak that Name out loud. It is firm Jewish tradition that only the high priest is to utter this name. And I think Christians should honor that tradition. So I will refer to "the Name," which is by and large how rabbis avoid it. No one has the slightest idea what, if anything, it means or where it came from. That is to say: it is a pure, personal, proper name. Why am I named Robert? Well, because when my parents named me it was not fashionable to give children Norwegian names. Robert sounded like a good Anglo-Saxon name and it seemed to fit. All that my name functions as is a reminder. It enables you to address me. Now as a matter of fact, my friends do not use the name "Robert" anymore. They just say "Jens." So if you want to be cozy with me, that is what you should say. Anyway, a name simply enables people to address each other. And that is the way the Name functions in Israel. It allows this people to address God.

Back to the story: after plagues and other things, the people escape by night and cross the boundary sea between Egypt and Sinai. There is one great battle with the pursuing Egyptian troops, in which the Israelites do not lift a finger. The Lord himself does all the work. So once again we see that God is deeply involved in the vicissitudes and triumphs of his people.

A whole book of the Bible—namely, Numbers—is devoted to Israel's new set of adventures with God. It is parallel to the story of Abraham, Isaac, and Jacob. What is important again is the picture of God wandering with his people through history. We must stop, however, at one place in their wanderings: the people came to Mt. Sinai.

As the story is told, there was a great, divine fireworks. Thunder, lightning, clouds, storms, and much else besides. And the whole people heard God speaking to them from the mountain. Then Moses crawled up to the mountain several times for a set of negotiations, the outcome of which is a covenant.

An ancient Near Eastern covenant was not an agreement but rather a unilaterally imposed treaty. At the heart of *this* covenant are two things: first, the Lord says to Israel, "I will be your God and you shall be my people." That double sentence will be Israel's maxim for its whole history. The second thing is the Ten Commandments, which is a brief summary of what a just and loving people would look like. No killing, no theft, no sexual infidelity, no envy, familial piety, and worshiping God. That is not a law in the sense that it is something you *have* to do. It is a law in the Jewish sense of *torah*. It is guidance—a display of what the good life would look like.

In the strength of this covenant, the Israelites finally make it out of the Sinai peninsula. Around 1000 BC, we find twelve

Israelite tribes occupying the land around the edges of which Abraham and his son and grandson had camped. Modern scholarship tends to doubt it. Some of them came from Egypt, but whether it was all twelve tribes or not is another question. However we decide that they came, when we find them there they are all worshiping the Lord. They all more or less acknowledge the Sinai covenant, and they all more or less acknowledge one another as allies in times of trouble. After a time, they adopt monarchy from the Canaanite cities around them, and with their first king, David, they even establish a small empire that covered most of modern-day Palestine and part of modern-day Lebanon, Syria, and Jordan. They have a great memory of the next King, Solomon, but then the empire breaks up into two states over issues of taxation. And so for most of its history, Israel is composed of two monarchies: a state in the north, Israel, and a state in the south, Judah.

The next big event after the establishment of these states is their undoing. Israel's northern kingdom was eventually destroyed by the Assyrians, which meant that its political and economic and military institutions were disbanded. The elites— the commercial, political, and military people—were carried off into exile. And so we have "the lost ten tribes of Israel." Now that is a stretch; it was only the elites of ten tribes of Israel who were lost. The common people of course remained right where they were. In 586, the Babylonians under King Nebuchadnezzar got tired of repeated insurrections and rebellions on the part of Judah, the southern kingdom, and came in force, besieged the city, took it, burned it to the ground, and carried off what was left of the southern elites to exile in Babylon. And that is the end of Israel as a politically independent entity. (Until, of course, it was resurrected in 1948. What to make theologically of that has not been settled either among Jews or Christians.)

Now in the religious history of the ancient world, such a catastrophe would normally have meant a discrediting of the god or gods of the nation that was destroyed. If Marduk could not save Babylon from the Persians, then what use is Marduk? In Israel, however, something strange happened.

Israel had been accustomed to prophets—that is, persons who claimed to have been sent by the Lord to speak the will of God in the lives of the people of Israel. I put it in this awkward fashion because Israel's prophets did not just *tell* the people of Israel the will of God. They came to *enforce* it. In about the middle of the eighth century and continuing then through the seventh century, and through the time of exile and for a time after the exile, a movement among the prophets arose proclaiming something religiously unprecedented: Israel's *own God*, they proclaimed, was responsible for their exile! Marduk could not have been responsible for undoing Babylon because if he was, there would not have been anything left of him! For when the Babylonians went under, Marduk went under with them. But these prophets insisted that the Lord God of Israel is so much God that even when his own people are undone, he is the one who has undone them. Now why had the Lord done this? The prophets involved in this movement said there were two reasons: one was the prevalence of injustice in the lives of Israelites. The lives of Israel, according to the prophets at least, were permeated with violence, false witness, adultery, theft, and so on. And second, idolatry. That is to say, if indeed the Lord was the specific God of this specific people, then they owed him their specific and unique loyalty. In fact, throughout their whole history until the exile, the people of Israel were characteristically quite happy to worship the Lord God so long as there were other gods to worship too. The most favorite other god among them was perhaps Astarte, a fertility goddess about whose practices you do not want to hear.

So for general religious and moral wickedness, the Lord had undone his own people. But there was another side to the prophets' message: after the punishment is complete, there will still be a remnant who had not followed the other gods. And indeed there was a remnant, the chief representative of which was the Israelites in captivity in Babylon. And the other side of these prophets' message was that God will act to restore Israel. And thereby the restoration of Israel's mission to the nations becomes more important than it had previously been. Abraham was called to create a nation that would be a blessing to the other nations. Now we find out in more detail what that means. The blessing of Israel to the nations would be to unify all nations in worship of the one God and so to establish universal peace. Nations will flock around Zion to be instructed in righteousness and, according to one of the prophets, to beat their swords into plowshares and their spears into pruning hooks.

As the prophets proclaimed this message, the promise to Abraham and the covenant mediated by Moses are then transformed in three ways. First, the blessing that Abraham's nation is to bring to the nations is ever more clearly proclaimed as the blessing of universal peace. And it becomes even more obvious that such universal peace is simply not possible within the way history now works. So with greater or lesser clarity, these prophets proclaim the coming of a whole new reality, a whole new heaven and earth, a whole new way in which history will work, a whole new justice and peace. When Jesus comes along, his name for this new reality will be the Kingdom of God or the Kingdom of Heaven—the day when the Lord's will for justice and peace will be done. Second, clearly only God can work this transformation. So for him to bring the kingdom where justice and peace will prevail, his involvement in history with his people will in the end have to be his unilateral work. He is going to have to do it himself. He cannot expect any help from Israel. And third, when this personal act of God in history reached this pitch of divine unilateralism, there arose various expectations of an identifiable human agent who will somehow be uniquely identified with the action of God. There were of course various ideas as to how this would happen. But somehow there would come a person whose actions will be the actions of God to bring the kingdom of God.

The kings of Israel were supposed to bring justice and peace but never did. The prophets of Israel had moreover promised this justice and peace. There will come a king from Israel, some people thought, who will bring peace and justice as the representative of God's own action. There will be a prophet of Israel, some people thought, who will not make Israel wait any longer. There will then come a prophet and a king who will do what prophets and kings were supposed to do and so far never had. Now the word that both later Judaism and Christianity made for all of these expectations was the word "Messiah" in Hebrew, which translates into Greek as "*Christos*" and is derived into English as "Christ."

Around 400 BC prophets were not popping up anymore and there was no king, good or bad. There was just a succession of empires coming and going to rule this little territory of Judah—first the Persians, then Alexander the Great, then the empires that succeeded Alexander the Great's empire when it broke up, and finally the Romans. There was no king, good or bad, but only overlords of one stripe or another. It looked to many as though the promises had failed. In the New Testament you will have encountered the Sadducees. They are the ones who had given up. They did not expect anything great anymore in the life of Israel. And then there are groups who had not given up. They are Pharisees and the Qumran sect. And there were violent revolutionaries. Barabbas, as you may have heard, belonged to one such group. All of them in their own ways had not yet given up.

3 | Jesus and Resurrection

There had been hundreds of years in which Israel had neither prophets nor kings. And then one day, a young man (and you must remember he was a young man), as Mark's Gospel says, simply came into Galilee—the northern part of what was left of Judah—proclaiming the good news of God. This young man, Jesus, immediately became a public figure.

The first thing to be said is that people did not know what in the world to make of Jesus. Modern historians are no different from Jesus's first followers in this regard. What we know of Jesus is what the Gospels tell of him. And they tell almost nothing of what psychologizers and gossipmongers would like to know. What did he look like? We have no clue. What color was he? We do not know. What was he doing for those thirty years before he popped up in Galilee proclaiming the good news of God? The Gospels say his father kept a carpenter shop. Did he ever have a girlfriend? We do not know. We do know he had a mother and we know her name. What the gospels mostly tell us is a great deal about what he said when he came preaching, somewhat less about what he did along the way of his preaching, and a long account of the events of his death.

If we venture to classify Jesus sociologically, we can start by calling him a wandering rabbi. Jesus went from place to place teaching, trailed by a crowd of disciples of greater or lesser degree of attachment to him. There was a circle of twelve who amounted to his family; they were his permanent students. And then there were others who were quite closely attached. We can read about a variety of them. There were people like Mary and Martha whom Jesus could count on for a bed and a meal when he was in the vicinity of Jerusalem. And then there were just crowds who would follow him for various lengths of time. Jesus traveled from place to place with this "wandering entourage," as we will now call it, teaching the Bible sometimes in synagogues, sometimes in houses, sometimes out in the open.

What astonished folk about Jesus? What made it impossible for people to know what to make of him? It was that he interpreted the scriptures as if he had written them. He interpreted them in a way that really only their author might be entitled to interpret them. People remarked that that he did not teach like the other rabbis, but "with authority"—that is, with the authority, with the power, with the entitlements that a living author would be expected to have in interpreting his own work.

Jesus also preached as a prophet. There had not been any prophets for a while, probably for around two hundred years. But now a couple of them had popped up. A man named John, who got the name "the baptizer" because when people came to hear his prophesy he would say "Repent! The kingdom of God is right around the corner and the axe is laid to the root of the tree. There is not much time left, folks!" And he would wash those who did repent in the river Jordan. And then there was Jesus. That passage at the beginning of Mark continues, "He came into Galilee proclaiming the good news of God." And it continues: "The time is fulfilled and ... the kingdom of God is at hand." The Greek word is "*eggiken*." "*Eggus*" means "there is no space left." The time is fulfilled; the kingdom of God is at hand. And then we find the same thing that John had said, "Believe this gospel, this good news." The phrase, "the kingdom of God" or "the kingdom of heaven," was Jesus's phrase for the new reality that Israel's prophecy had proclaimed. So as far as content was concerned Jesus had very little new to say; he picked right up where the other prophets had left off.

Apparently, Jesus did this preaching and teaching mostly by parables. That is to say, he told stories that picked up some common feature of life and twisted it in an odd fashion. So, for example, he said in one of his most famous parables: "The kingdom of God is like a sower who went out to plant a field and scattered the seed. Some of it fell on good ground; some of it fell on the highway; some of it fell on the thorns. And what fell on the good ground grew, but the rest of it did not grow." And then he shut up. Now what is so strange about this story is that no farmer would sow a field that way. I mean, can you imagine a farmer just going down the highway sowing seed on the concrete? So what kind of a farmer is the farmer of the kingdom of God? How would God farm his kingdom? That is the question, you see, that is posed by this parable. Jesus taught mostly by parables, which were partly intended to be easy to understand and partly intended to be mysterious.

What was new? Even parables had been regularly used by the old prophets—not to the extent that Jesus used them, but they had been used. What was new was not the content of Jesus's prophesying. What was new was that his proclamation of the immediate coming of the kingdom of God left people no time to get ready. The old prophets had always left people with time to get ready. Jesus's prophesying left people with no time at all. Those who heard him either had to accept the message or turn it down. In effect, a person's acceptance or rejection of the kingdom of God's immanent arrival was consonant with their reaction to Jesus himself. Now a rabbi who taught the Old Testament (or the *Tanakh*) as if he had written it, and who proclaimed the coming of the kingdom of God in such fashion that your acceptance or rejection of the message was identical with your acceptance or rejection of him, what was one to make of that? "Was he the Messiah," people asked? Whether Jesus himself thought he was the Messiah is a subject over which scholars have disputed since the New Testament was written. It is a matter on which they are not likely to come to a definitive solution.

He was, however, executed as a messianic pretender. The Jewish and the Roman authorities suspected him of being someone who *would* proclaim himself the Messiah. Evidently they did not want to hear anything like that because then the Jewish religious authorities could be refuted. And then the Romans might have an insurrection on their hands. So over his gallows, as was customary, the Roman authorities put a plank with the charge written on it. What was Jesus executed for doing? Supposedly, what was written there was "Jesus of Nazareth, the king of the Jews." He refused all earthly power, though it would have been available to him. It was quite clear in those last days in Jerusalem that if Jesus had wanted to start an insurrection, he could have done it. And though he refused all use of earthly power, people could not get over feeling some sort of "absolute authority" in his words and in his actions.

And finally, he was a healer—a rabbi, a prophet, and a healer. Some of the stories of Jesus's healings are quite straightforward;

others are quite bizarre. It seems past historical dispute that the historical Jesus of Nazareth did heal people. His healings were, according to the Gospels, done not as sort of proofs that he could do it but as signs, acted-out parables of what the kingdom of God would be like. This kingdom of God that he claimed was so close at hand would be a place where the lame walked, the demon possessed were cured, and so on.

Those who had hoped that Jesus was the Messiah were completely let down by his execution. The Messiah was not supposed to die. Still less was he to be executed by the Romans; he was supposed to *defeat* the Romans. The reason that the Gospels spent so much time on Jesus's death was that it had to be explained. And the way the Gospels explain it is by telling every detail of the story in such a fashion that it refers back to the Old Testament. Jesus cannot be thirsty without reference to thirst in the Old Testament. If the Roman soldiers swipe his clothes, this is told by way of reading citations from a Psalm, and so forth and so forth. In effect, the Gospels identify the death of Jesus with the death of Israel.

Now we must look a little more closely at the way death figures in the Scriptures. The difference between a live person and a dead person or between a live community and a dead community can be summed up this way: a live person or a community has a future; a dead person or community does not. And therefore death must be the opposite and the enemy of the God who is portrayed in Israel's memory of its own history. I have been insisting that the God portrayed in Israel's historical memory is a God who is active in that history. Now to be active at something is to be aiming at something. To be active in history as opposed to simply inhabiting it is, in a famous phrase of twentieth-century theology, "to be open to a future"—to be aiming at, to be grasped by, what is not yet. When you hear people say that they want to live in the present, the only answer to that is, "Well, where else do you suppose you would be living?" Sometimes, they mean that they want to live in the present just *for* the present. But the only way to do that would be to be dead. They would be living for the present, having no relationship to the future. To be in history is precisely *not* to be dead; it is precisely *not* to lack a future.

The God portrayed in the Old Testament, in Israel's memory of its life, is the God who is active in history. Another favorite way of characterizing that God in Scripture and in the church's tradition is to say that he is "the living God." That is to say that God has a future toward which he aims, and that he involves those who involve themselves with him in that same future. That Israel lives with the God that she has means that she is open to a future. It means that she is supposed to be going someplace, aiming at someplace, some promise given to Abraham. Thus God and death are flatly opposed to each other in Israel's understanding of things.

That is not religiously common. Think for example of the religion of ancient Egypt where the dead and the gods are very nearly identified with each other, where the way to become a god is by dying. That is not how Israel saw its God. And because its God and death were opposed to each other, through most of its history Israel hardly knew what to think about death. Through most of Israel's history it got along by finessing the matter. For Israel, like all nations, more or less assumed its own immortality. Americans can conceive of America losing its power. We can conceive of America being defeated. We can conceive of America being broke. But we cannot really conceive of a world without America full stop. Nations just assume their own immortality, and Israel did the same. And so long as individual Israelites identified themselves closely with the community, then the immortality of the community sufficed. I may die, but what I really am is just one link in the chain of Israelites and I will live on in the continuance of the nation. But in Israel's case, this assumption of national immortality could be challenged. For Israel knew something that other nations by and large will not admit: that it had a beginning.

There was a time before Abraham when there was not any Israel and when the world had gotten along. So there could be a time when there was not any Israel any longer, and the world would continue. Because Israel knew that its beginning had been an act of God within history, it knew also that it could come to an end within history. And if it forgot this, the prophets were there to remind it. When the people of Israel returned from the exile, they formed a tiny religious community ruled by other people. The exile seemed to have brought Israel to its end. Thus the Lord's question to Ezekiel, "Has death won?" The Lord answers by commanding Ezekiel to prophesy the dead Israelites back to life. Ezekiel obeys. And indeed the dead bones hear the word of the Lord.

Looking back at the beginning of Israel's history, one can see that something like this was going to be the inevitable turning point. The Israelites followed and worshiped the God who was the enemy of death. Yet death was a predominant reality in which the Israelites lived. And indeed the sketch of Israel's life that I gave was plotted to show that. From this point of view, Israel's history leads to a climactic confrontation between Israel's God and death. And so Israel's question is really the question that every people eventually asks: "Does death win? Does life have any other point than its own refutation?" What happened to Israel from one point of view, then, was the historical outworking of the question of all questions. Martin Heidegger, the greatest and most wicked philosopher of the twentieth century, built the whole structure of his thought on the message that what it means for me to be a human being fulfills itself precisely in that I not only die, but live my whole life doing nothing but affirming my oncoming death. In any case, the question posed to Ezekiel by the outcome of Israel's history with God is the same question at the heart of the history of Western philosophy—especially modernity: "Does death win?" The Christian church claims that Jesus's resurrection is the Lord's own answer to this question.

So, what does this resurrection then look like? Two sorts of events are described: his tomb is found empty, and his former disciples meet him in various situations. Now at this point, some initial skepticism is surely called for. And indeed the Gospels seem to be perfectly aware of that. As the Gospels tell the story, one of Jesus's own disciples did not at first believe that Jesus could actually be alive. The ancients, you see, were no more prejudiced on the matter than we moderns. If anything, the opposite is the case. After all, you do not need to be a molecular biologist to know that the dead do not customarily pop back up again! You do not need an electron microscope to ascertain that irreversible molecular changes are taking place in a corpse; all you need is your nose. The fact that the tomb was empty was a shock. Nor was it taken as proof of Jesus's resurrection. Somebody could simply have moved the body. And that indeed is the story that the Roman authorities put out. They lost the body of this notorious prisoner or else it had been swiped.

On the other hand, the resurrection appearances—at meals, on the road, in a little assembly of disciples hiding out from the police—are another matter. If you meet someone, you are inclined to suppose that he is alive—unless, of course, you are superstitious and expect to run into ghosts or ectoplasmic manifestations. Those determined to think that Jesus stayed dead have throughout the centuries adduced various theories for explaining the so-called resurrection appearances. The disciples are said to have shared a mass hallucination, or to have formed a conspiracy to make up the story, and the like. But as the most philosophically sophisticated German-speaking theologian of my generation, Wolfhart Pannenberg, pointed out: there is absolutely no evidence for any such hypothesis. The only ground on which such theories rest is the determination *not* to believe that Jesus has risen. Consider the conspiracy theory. If you belong to a movement whose leader had just been executed for political reasons and you were in hiding lest you suffer the same fate, it would not occur to you to come bursting out into public and try to tell people that he is really alive. That is not what you would think to do.

Pannenberg went so far as to say that Jesus's resurrection is the only historically plausible proposition that covers the evidence. I think that goes too far, but I think it is clear that there is no evidential basis for its denial either. *Here* is the point at which this alleged piece of news either grabs you or it does not. If it does grab you, if you believe Jesus was raised, Christians will attribute this to the Holy Spirit.

If the accounts of the resurrection are anywhere near correct—that is, if people were in fact meeting this Jesus who had been dead for three days—then Jesus was not resuscitated.

That is to say, whatever happened to him it is not analogous to what happens to people whose hearts have stopped for a long time and suddenly start beating again. Jesus was not resuscitated. Although the tomb was thought to be empty and though his resurrection as was promised to Ezekiel is a bodily resurrection (this is not a ghost, not a pure spirit, but somebody with a body), that body is very strangely related to time and space. Where is he between appearances? It is quite clear that he was not checked into the Jerusalem Hilton. He is not hanging out, waiting to come and show himself again. When he meets one of those who see him, from where does he come to them? Nor is this body impeded spatially as we are. One of the most central stories depicts Jesus suddenly appearing to his disciples in a locked room. Did he walk through the door? Or was the door there not "there" for Jesus in the same way as it was for his disciples? We will come back to the metaphysics later on. However we work them out, we will need to say how Jesus's resurrected body is related to time and space.

In any case, the meaning of this event would have been plain to any Jew who had been reading the Old Testament. If God has raised someone from the dead, then two things are going to be plain to any pious Jew: first, the resurrection of the dead that was promised to Ezekiel has begun. As the rest of the New Testament is sometimes going to put it, Jesus is the forerunner, the pioneer, the way-breaker of the general resurrection of the dead. Second, the pioneer of resurrection can be called the Messiah. Again, whether Jesus thought he was the Messiah is a matter of scholarly dispute. But he must be if he was in fact raised from the dead. So the chief reality of the resurrection is not that something remarkable happened once upon a time. Of course, if Jesus was in fact raised, then something remarkable did happen. But the truly important thing is that this particular Jewish rabbi, healer, and prophet who people had hoped would be the Messiah now lives. And not only that. His life is embodied such that when Christians observe the Lord's Supper, or the Eucharist, or Communion (or whatever a particular denomination wants to call it), they gather around the body of Christ.

So the disciples are in possession of information that the Messiah has come and lives and lives embodied. Those who came to think that he was indeed raised—those who met him in a body—are in possession of information that is vital news for all. And so with absolutely appalling *hutzpah*, they set out to tell everybody. And in this they are again following Old Testament expectations. The nations would be gathered in to the worship of the one Lord God by the Messiah. A few people believed them and handed the story on.

So if Jesus was not between appearances hanging out in the local pub, where was he? This risen body of Christ, where was it? For that matter, where *is* it? There is a two-part answer. The New Testament itself suggests that Jesus comes to meet his disciples "from heaven." And the Christian Creed in its second article says, "On the third day he rose again and ascended into heaven." What is heaven? Well, the word is used in the Scriptures for a variety of things. But maybe you can boil down the Scriptures' talk about heaven in this way: if God is not just outside time and space but rather involved in the doings of time and space, then he needs his own place within space, within creation. Irreverently put, heaven is God's pad in his creation.

Once upon a time before Copernicus, this did not cause any conceptual difficulty. The best science at the time provided precisely a place for God. As you know, the Ptolemaic system thought of the earth as this little plot in the middle surrounded by crystalline spheres. The farther you got from earth, the purer and more glorious things became. Heaven, then, is the outermost sphere. From any point on earth, therefore, you get to heaven by ascending. Now this was not crude; this was the best science at the time. And if this seems quaint to us, just think of what our science will look like two thousand years from now. It will look just as quaint. So there was no conceptual problem. Nor was there a problem with Christ's Ascension. Jesus appeared off and on to his disciples for a period of forty days and then ascended. That is to say, he went back to heaven, from which he had been coming all along, and stayed there. And as to how he got there, he escalated. There are stained glass windows all over Europe which show the disciples gathered around in a little circle and there is a cloud with a pair of little feet dangling out of the bottom. That produces a giggle now, but it did not at the time. People think that the problem with Copernicus was that he demoted the world from being the center of everything; that is not the problem. In the Ptolemaic system the world was indeed at the center, but that meant it was the thickest, dullest, part of the universe. The farther away you got, the better things became.

Theology was compelled to a decided, fundamental rethinking of God's place within creation by the Copernican system. And there are two sides of the rethinking: one is to conceive heaven not spatially, but temporally. Heaven is that future toward which God aims, the kingdom of God. Heaven is that future toward which God wills to bring his people insofar as Jesus is already present with God. So, spatially, where is heaven? I answer: wherever God is. To say that God points to a future is not to say that he is lacking something and trying to catch up with it. The future toward which God points is always already present with him. And heaven is that future to which he wills to bring his people insofar as it is already present with him. So the Christian Creed says, "Ascended into heaven and sits at the right hand of the Father." That is to say, heaven is the right hand of the Father; heaven is wherever God's power extends. When God comes to us, he comes from where he wants to bring us. And that "from" is heaven.

The other side of the rethinking compelled by Copernicus regards a conception of what it means to say that someone has a body. If Christ was raised in the body, where is that body? Well, it is in the future. What does that mean? What is a body? To say that Christ was raised in the body is not to say that there is necessarily an organism somewhere that looks like Jesus of Nazareth. What, then, do we mean by saying that someone is or has a body? Suppose that I were disembodied before you in the middle of this lecture. What would happen? Let us suppose that the thoughts that constitute this lecture continued to emerge in your head. What would you be missing when you missed now the body of Jenson, but not the subject, Jenson? You would not be able to get at me. Supposing that what emerged in your head was so offensive that you wanted to throw me out of the room, where would you find me? Or suppose that what emerged in your head was so great that you wanted to kiss me, how would you manage that? You see, the "existential" reality of a body is its availability. My body is simply me insofar as I am available to you, insofar as you can get at me. You can see me. You can touch me. If you get close, you can catch my cold. The body of the risen Christ, then, is fundamentally whatever it is by which he is available to us. So when we say in the Christian church that the bread on the table of the Lord's Supper is the body of Christ, we do not mean that it is a chunk of an organism. We mean that it is something available and that this is where the risen Christ is encountered.

4 | The Triune God

The church believes that the God of Israel had raised one of his servants, Jesus of Nazareth, from the dead, and that the consequences of that are earth- and life-shaking news for anyone who listened. So the church was from the beginning a missionary movement, first among Jews and then among gentiles as well. For part of what they thought followed from the resurrection was that the time promised in the Old Testament had come: Abraham's blessing should be extended outside the children of Israel.

In the missionary situation, theological questions immediately arise, since gentile converts come with a set of theological maxims, cultural habits, and religious practices already ingrained in them. When they are captivated by Jesus, they carry these previous commitments with them. And out of this, questions arise that need answering. In fact, they need answering so desperately that they regularly provoke knockdown arguments.

The question and controversy before us now break out in AD 150. They so drastically disturbed the young church that it did not really come to any kind of resolution until AD 381. And to some extent the debate is still going on. The accumulation of more or less agreed results to date is generally known as the doctrine of the Trinity. That doctrine is regarded as Christianity's big, difficult thing. Father, Son, and Holy Spirit count one, two, three and yet there is only one God. How do you work that out?

Let me say more about the missionary context in which this question came about. Again, the church became quickly convinced that the resurrection was a signal that the time had come to begin gathering the gentiles. And with gentile converts an inevitable feature of the missionary situation begins. Converts come with antecedent convictions. The missionary impulse begins of course at Jerusalem, which is where the Jewish church was, and it goes both east and west. So it goes into the world of the Mediterranean basin, the world that had been hellenized by the conquest of Alexander the Great. The missionary impulse went west into the Hellenistic world and east into the Near East and beyond. There is not much left of the church that was founded by the eastern missionaries as a result of Islamic conquest in the seventh century. The present-day churches in Asia are not the original Asian churches for the most part. They are the result of Western missionaries. So it is chiefly the Hellenistic world that we are interested in.

Hellenistic converts came with a drastically different construal of the being of God than the one found in the Old Testament. Most people of course had not read Plato or Aristotle, but if they had any schooling they had teachers who told them about Plato or Aristotle. The Greek thinkers had construed God's being as precisely immunity to and distance from what goes on in time and history. What makes God God for Plato or Aristotle is precisely that it—you can hardly say "he," you have to say "it"—is unaffected by anything going on in time. So Aristotle's God is a pure act of thought (not even a mind because there is no material substrata) the content of which is simply itself. It is an act of thinking about thinking. What makes that a good thing to have around? It pays no attention to us, so why should we pay attention to it? Because it is a sort of anchor from the vicissitudes of time. The way out of the mess of this world is to become just a little bit like this God and, thus, to forget about what happens to me or what I am called upon to do, and instead rest in my own self-consciousness.

That is a very different construal of God's being or—put it this way—of the relationship between time and eternity than is found in the Old Testament. In this conception, God's eternity is not that he rules over time as it is in the Old Testament. The eternity of God is rather that he is remote from and uninterested in time. This theology had been spread over the Mediterranean by the cultural dominance of the Greeks. Those who became somehow hooked on the Israelites and Jesus, then, were confronted by a great cognitive dissonance. They came to believe that stories are true about God that could not possibly be true about him if God were the way Hellenistic culture said he is. God rescued Israel from Egypt except that that cannot possibly be true if God is uninterested in places like Egypt and Israel. This cognitive dissonance gives rise to a first spurt of what you might call academic theology within the Christian church. Paul was not a teacher; he was a missionary. Matthew, Mark, Luke, and John were not professors; they were people desperately trying to remember what there was to remember about Jesus. But from around AD 150 on, you have folk like me: people committed to the Christian message whose calling is the classroom.

Two attempts to resolve this cognitive dissonance emerged very early. Historians call the first attempt Modalism. That is the position of people who said that God is somewhat like Plato and Aristotle say he is. He is not personally involved in time. He certainly does not go around getting crucified on a cross. Father, Son, and Spirit, they said, are different modes in which this transcendent, timeless God reveals himself. This was the first piece of theoretical theology in the history of the Christian faith. Then around AD 150, another proposal was advanced by people we call the Apologists.

The Apologists were people with a little (or in some cases quite a lot) of Hellenistic education who undertook to explain to their fellow Hellenists how the Father, Son, and Holy Spirit are one. Their solution is called the "Logos theology." The Greek word "logos" can be translated either as "word" or "reason," but the word itself means both at once. In this conception, I have an idea, a *logos*, a thought, an act of reasoning, and I express that in language. The act of reason and the act of speech are simultaneous. Even if you don't speak your thought out loud you speak it to yourself insofar as language and thinking are inseparable. Greek thinkers spoke of "*the* Logos," the reason inherent in God insofar as it is expressed. The expression is the rationality we can find in the world. Although the world is a mess and ultimate salvation is a matter of getting out of it by finding refuge in the timeless being of God, Greek thinkers nevertheless held that the world does make some sense. Water always does run downhill. Two and two always make four. The Pythagorean theorem always holds, and so forth and so on. There are definitive patterns of nature that can be thought; we can grasp the *logos* in them.

The Logos, then, is God's own rationality insofar as it is expressed in the rationality of the world. Now, the Apologists thought this idea was exactly the kind of thing they needed to make the Christian God intelligible to their fellow Hellenists. What is it exactly that has happened with Jesus? The rationality of God, the Logos, has come to inhabit him. God himself is uninvolved with this world and its processes, but his Logos—precisely because it is the rationality expressed in the world—is nevertheless at home here. If, then, the Logos comes to inhabit a particular human being, as he does with Jesus, then we have a solution to the apparent dissonance between God's timeless eternity and the Incarnation. In Jesus, the Logos can involve himself in history while God himself does not need to.

Neither of these solutions could work in the long run because both do something that Scripture does not permit. They construe an entity that is almost God, but not quite. With respect to Modalism, the three modes in which God is said to appear are merely God's *manifestations* within history and time. They are not God himself. What was the problem with Logos theologies?

To answer this question, I want to draw your attention to a man named Origen who lived in the early part of the third century. He was Christianity's first world-class intellectual and, indeed, one of the greatest intellectuals of the ancient world, Christian or otherwise. Origen created an entire system around the Logos theology which, for nearly a century, was simply assumed by teachers and preachers who had any education at all. But though Origen's system seemed to work, there was a contradiction hidden in it. The extraordinary sophistication of Origen's thinking could hide this contradiction for a while, but not forever. In Scripture—and Origen as the first great scholarly exegete of Scripture dug his own grave at this point—there are just two kinds of being: there is the Creator and then there are creatures. Whereas the Hellenistic world was full of intermediary beings, the world of Scripture speaks of nothing but God and creatures.

So which is this Logos? Half-Gods and half-creatures are not to be found in the Bible. If He is on the Creator side, then the Logos theology reproduces the problem it was supposed to solve. If He is on the creature side, then how can he save us? What then did it matter that Jesus suffered on our behalf? If The Logos is just a creature, then he needs to be saved with all of the rest of us. That was the contradiction hidden in Origen's system and in all predecessor Logos theologies from the start. You might say that the Logos is 99.99 percent God but not 100 percent God, that he is God's own rationality and yet not fully divine. The Apologists effectively reduced Christ and the Spirit to the "almost-gods"— the semi-semi-semi gods of pagan antiquity.

This contradiction was kept hidden by a fancy conceptual double-talk. But then the thing blew up on account of a literal-minded priest from Alexandria named Arius who made the contradiction explicit. Arius insisted that if Christ the Logos can be crucified, then he is a creature—a very special creature, a creature so much like God that you can take him for God—but nevertheless a creature. Arius made Christ a creature whom Christians worship. But that is the precise biblical definition of idolatry. Thus, for saying what he said Arius got fired by his bishop. Arius then appealed to the like-minded among the clergy of the eastern church, and he was soon defended by other bishops. Soon bishops were excommunicating each other all over the map.

Significantly, it was just at this moment that Constantine looked to the newly liberated church to provide a unifying moral structure to hold the empire together. Paganism could no longer do it. "Christianity," thought Constantine, "is the religion of love. Perhaps Christian love as inculcated in the Christian congregations can provide the moral cement needed to hold the empire together." So he looked to the newly liberated church to provide a unity in love as a moral foundation for the empire. What he found instead was a church in a fight among its own that was being conducted in grossly unloving ways.

Constantine summoned the bishops of the church together to a town called Nicea that is just across the water from Istanbul. He sat them down and said, "Settle this. Get over it. Find some way you can agree." After months of argument the bishops came up with a solution that is not exactly what one would hope for from Christian theology. They wrote a decree they knew Arius could not sign. They did not necessarily know what they meant by some of the language that they used. But they did know that Arius had contradicted it. Today, Christians use a later version of that creed called the Nicene-Constantinopolitan creed. In it, we hear that the Logos is "God from God," "true God from true God," "begotten, not made," which is to say not a creature. And then there is the famous phrase, "*homoousioun to patri*," which the usual modern English translation of the Nicene Creed renders "of one being with the Father." That is to say, whatever is involved in being God is identical for the Father and the Son. Again, no one exactly knew what *homoousios to patri* meant. If you were to grab some of those bishops and ask what does *homoousios* mean, you would have just gotten a stutter.

As one might have expected, the tactics that had been used to form the Nicene Creed did not in fact produce peace. On the contrary, the controversy became more severe after Nicea than it had been before. It made the division worse between those who supported the results of the Council of Nicaea and those who rejected them. And those who rejected them did so for two reasons. One, they regarded the council as having overthrown and criticized the theological tradition in which all of them had been raised. Nobody likes to change his mind, and the Council of Nicaea called on two thirds of the clergy and teachers of the church to abandon the whole way of thinking they had learned and adopt a new way. Second, the key term of the Council of Nicaea's alleged solution turns on the phrase "homoousios." And people rightly asked, "What do you mean by that?" and were regularly faced with "I do not know, but it sounds well, does it not?"

So the fight went on until the second great Council at Constantinople in 381. What had happened in the meantime was two things. First, a theologian named Athanasius had proposed an interpretation of that word "homoousios" which, whether you liked it or not, at least made some sense. He said that the Father and the Son, the first and second persons of the Trinity, are the same God precisely in virtue of the *relationship* between them. Precisely in the form of his relationship to God the Father, the Logos is the same God as God the Father. Now to make that work, you have to do something which has remained within Western thinking ever since and, in fact, at the moment is very much in vogue. You have to think of reality as more constituted in the relationships between things than in the things themselves. So the Father is God precisely because he is related to the Son. The Son is the same God precisely because he is related to the Father. It is the relationship that is the metaphysically heavy fact rather than the poles of the relationship.

Second, a group of younger theologians, three of them—all related—called the Cappadocians had worked out a system of thought as sophisticated as Origen's. They said the Christian God is one being in three "*hypostases*," the best English equivalent for which is "identities." There is in God, said the Cappadocians, just one being, which is why there is just one God. The is-ness of God is single, but there are three hypostases. A hypostasis is something that can be identified, or even you might say a hypostasis simply is an identity. So there is something up here yacking away at you people; there is being, the being of Jenson, and then there is an identity. Somebody can ask you, "Well who is that up there?" and you can answer in various ways—for example, the funny guy with the beard, the professor of this class, Robert W. Jenson, a refugee from teaching theologians, and so on. Now there are three identities of the one being of God. Who is this God? Well, he is God the author of the story with his people. Who is this God? He is God settled into that story and an actor in it. Who is God? He is the wind of God that moves history. Or in the language that came to be standard, Father, Son, and Holy Spirit. And any one of them is a perfect and complete identification of the one God.

In my view, the Cappadocian intuition is the basis for the most satisfying view—which is to say, the most *biblical*—formulation of the doctrine of the Trinity. To explain this point we need to reconsider a widespread misconception. It is often supposed that Christian trinitarianism is a total break from Judaism's understanding of God. The Jews are said to have the doctrine that there is only one God and the Christians are said to have introduced a modification. This is historically false, and two of the most profound contemporary Jewish theologians, Michael Wyschogrod and Peter Ochs, both recognize that. Neither Judaism nor Christianity is an abstract monotheist religion. Neither insists that there is just one God and that this is all that can be said about him. Both are rather instances of what I would like to call "dramatic monotheism." For both Judaism and Christianity, the oneness of God is the oneness of the story that he lives with his people.

I have been insisting from the outset that the God of Israel himself lives his history with his people. Now, if this is a history and not just chaos, then it must have a plot. It cannot just be a random sequence of events; it must be dramatically coherent. It must hang together in the way that a play does. If the story that the God of Israel lives with his people has a plot, if it is going somewhere and has turning points and so forth, it must also have a cast of characters or dramatis personae. If you look at the Old Testament, it is fairly easy to identify these personae, these characters of the play, these persons of the plot. On Israel's and humanity's side there is a multitude. But on God's side, the cast is quite limited and fairly clearly to be seen.

There is, first, the Lord of Israel who rules Israel's history as its author, who in some sense stands outside of the play or drama as the author of the drama. And then there is God himself as a figure *in* the drama, a figure *in* the history of Israel. Consider, for example, "the angel of the Lord." Throughout the Pentateuch when something really decisive happens, the *"malach yhwh"*— that is, the angel or messenger of the Lord—appears to speak on the Lord's behalf. As the tale goes on, however, this angel or messenger of the Lord speaks *as* God in the first person. It turns out that he *is* the Lord. So the *malach* of the Lord is simultaneously a messenger *for* the Lord or *of* the Lord but also the Lord himself. Or there is "the glory" of the Lord. In the temple of Jerusalem we find simultaneously a manifestation of the Lord, the glory

of the Lord, and a sort of shining of the Lord which just *is* the
Lord. We could go on. The old rabbis of somewhere between 150
BC to AD 300 regarded such phenomena as different forms of the
same thing which they called the "*shekinah,*" which means "the
settlement one" or "the resident one." The *shekinah* of God, then,
is God as resident within the life of Israel as distinguished from
God as author and transcendent to the life of Israel.

And then finally on this list of characters there is the spirit of
the Lord. The Hebrew says *ruah,* which means wind or breath.
The Old Testament is full of references to and appearances of the
ruah of God, the breath of God by which he blows things around
and so keeps Israel's history moving. Whenever things seem to
come to a halt—if the Philistines, say, have once again got Israel
stymied—the same thing happens again and again. The *ruah* of
the Lord falls upon so and so, and thus takes over and rescues
Israel. That is to say, it is the wind of God's own life blowing on
history that keeps it moving.

Thus far we have the dramatis personae, the characters of the
story that the Lord has with his people Israel. You will notice
there are three. The only change worked by the resurrection is
the claim that the *shekinah*, the indwelling of God within the
story of his people, has appeared in permanent form as one
individual Israelite. It was taken as a conclusion from the resurrection of Jesus that he was and is the *shekinah*. So the dramatis personae are God as the author, but also Jesus Christ as the
indwelling of God in that story, and the Spirit as the breath of
God as the *dynamis*, the agitation of that story.

The result in the text of the New Testament is a phenomenon
that I have sometimes labeled "primary trinitarianism." The
New Testament writers, particularly the epistle writers, St. Paul

above all, but also the writer of Acts and other New Testament writers, are scarcely able to talk about God without mentioning each of the three dramatis personae each time they do.

Now that is the root and substance and heart of the so-called doctrine of the Trinity. God has a history with his people and the personages of this history are the Father of Jesus who is the author of the story, Jesus Christ, and the Spirit. It—the doctrine of the Trinity, I mean—is moreover the root and substance of the prayer that Jesus taught his disciples to pray. Jesus said to start off this way: "Our Father"; and then he gave them the prayer which was a traditional Jewish prayer except for something new at the beginning. We translate "Father," but the Aramaic word that he would have used was *Abba*, which is the Aramaic equivalent of "Daddy" or "Papa." That is to say, Jesus taught his disciples to address God as their daddy and then to bring their concerns to God as his children. Now, calling God "Father" in a general sort of way is a thing that pops up normally. But calling him "Our Father" as a way to begin prayer—now nobody did that; that was the new thing. How do Christians dare do that? I mean what in the world gives me the right every day to start off a prayer "Dear Daddy?" It is the "our" in there that counts. Jesus himself always addressed God this way. And Jesus invited his disciples to piggyback on his own relationship to God. So we pray to Jesus's Father with him, with the Son, and in the Spirit who is the spiritual energy by which or whom we hope to do that. In this respect the whole doctrine of the Trinity can be explained by simply remarking that Christians pray to the Father, with the Son, in the Spirit, and are convinced that by so doing they are properly caught up in the story that God lives with his people.

5 | Creation

In any standard, full presentation of Christian doctrine, the one that comes after the doctrine of God, which is what we just went on about, is the doctrine of Creation. And for no better reason than the usual standard order, that is what we at this point take up next here.

The church at this point simply took over the Jewish doctrine, the standard teaching of Judaism of Jesus's time. The Lord, Judaism said, created the heavens and the earth as in the first verse of Genesis: "In the beginning God created the heavens and the earth," meaning everything. The Lord created the heavens and the earth and he did so out of nothing. There is a phrase you will hear, "ex nihilo," Latin for "out of nothing." That is to say, there is God and there is everything else and there is nothing but those two. Moreover, the existence of the latter, the "everything else," depends entirely upon the choice of the former, God, that it shall be. Ex nihilo: there is nothing but God and what he chooses to exist and therefore there was nothing for him to work on antecedently. God did not manufacture out of materials at hand or give birth to the world or whatever. There is God and there is everything else and there is nothing but these two, and the existence of the latter depends entirely upon the choice of the former that it shall be. If God ceased in this instance actively to choose

my existence, I would not be and—what is more—I would never
have been.

Moreover, since the creation thus depends on an act of the
creator—he *chooses* that the world shall be—the creation has a
beginning. There was when it was not, then God chose that it
should be, and it is. If only we had the necessary information, we
could therefore count back to a time "zero" of the world—if you
like, to a "big bang." Theologians like very much the "big bang"
variety of cosmology; they do not like the slow sizzle variety very
much. This does not mean, however, that there is a single timeline on which the creation appears at one point. Time is itself
created. It is an old joke; somebody is supposed to have asked
Augustine what God was doing before he created the world and
the answer was that he was making a hell for people who asked
stupid questions. Asking about a "time" before the creation is
a category mistake; it is a stupid question, a question that cannot be answered. So, a la Einstein, time and space are characters
of the world that actually exists, which is why Christian theologians who tend to like Einstein are not quite as happy about
some varieties of quantum theory. The timeline on which the
creation appears is itself created. Creation and creation's time
are created together. It is a simple proposition, but it is hard to
visualize because we always keep on wanting to ask what was
going on *before*.

Now, this doctrine was Israel's mature doctrine. It only
appeared in this strict and conceptualized form toward the very
end of old Israel's history. And it is a very particular answer
to a perennial question. Indeed all religions are in one respect
an answer to this question, which, in the modern period, was
most sharply formulated by that wicked twentieth-century

philosopher, Martin Heidegger. He wrote a little book—it is a very good little book—called *Introduction to Metaphysics*. The first sentence is, "Warum gibt es überhaupt etwas und nicht vielmehr nichts?"—Why is there anything at all? Why not just nothing?" How are we to understand the sheer existence of all this stuff, including us? Israel and its derivatives—that is to say, Judaism, Christianity, and Islam—give a very religiously peculiar answer. Indeed, it is a decisive criticism of the answers given by the rest of the world's religions.

Probably the most profound and in any case the most widespread answer to that question "Warum gibt es überhaupt?" is to construe the reality of the world on the analogy of sexual intercourse and birth. Birth is after all humanity's one great experience of something coming to be there that was not there before, of the genuine emergence of the new. And once people have observed that in the case of humanity itself, of course there are analogs all over the place. It does not take a molecular biologist to notice that the plants need to be fertilized. You have to have the bees if you are going to have any flowers, fruit, and so forth. So, out from the union of two emerges a something new. By and large, the two in the great systems of religion are "Father Sky" and "Mother Earth." Father Sky rains on Mother Earth, that is to say, his semen showers down and Mother Earth becomes pregnant, and the world is born of their union. Now that of course implies that somehow or other sky and earth were there before the world, and that is a decisive feature of most of the religions in answer to that question "Why is there anything at all?" The answer that is given suggests a sort of eternal pansexuality.

Creation accounts that appeal to the model of sex and birth are marked by four features. First, there has to be something scenically there for the birth to come from. Creation is not out of nothing; it is out of an antecedent male and an antecedent female eternal principle. Second, what is born is always somehow like what it is born from. It may take a while in the case of many insects, but sooner or later from butterflies come butterflies. And that is to say this eternal male-female whatever and the world are fundamentally the same. If I can now switch to language like this, the world is like the divine from which it is born. The world is like the divine, only just less so. And that means that there is always something lacking about the world. It is like the eternal sexuality from which it was born, but it is not that. It is like the divine; it is 90 percent divine, but it is not as divine as that from which it comes. In the third place, notice that there is no real *creating* going on (that is a distinctively Jewish idea). There is no *creating* but only *birthing*. There is rather the eternal or the divine sex pair—you cannot think of them as *a* male and *a* female but rather as eternal maleness and femaleness—and, then, whatever results from their union. The Greek conception of emanation is just a more conceptually sophisticated version of this narrative: the world emanates from some eternal divine principle like a baby from a mother, like light from sun, like stream from the spring. The metaphors here pile up that the world pours forth from. There is not a creator because there is no creating going on; there is just emanation. The fourth feature hinges on necessity. The eternal sexuality *must* produce offspring. Father Sky and Mother Earth, to use the morphological language, do not decide to have at it one day; that is just the way it is, which is why there is something rather than nothing.

The second model is much less profound. It answers the question of why there is anything rather than nothing by invoking the notion of a great cosmic victory. Before there is the world, there is God, and there is a sort of anti-world, chaos. The Babylonian story is a good one to illustrate this. Before there was the world there were the gods, and the hero of the gods is a guy named Marduk. And then there is the great slimy monster, a huge everything in general and nothing in particular, a disorganized but just so malevolent sort of dragon. Now there is an empirical basis for that sort of picture. Marduk is the God of Babylon and Babylon is in the southern part of the territory between the Tigris and Euphrates rivers, and apart from drainage ditches and irrigation works, that whole part of the world simply would be one great big slime. And then one day Marduk slew Tiamat and divided her body—sorry about that, but the chaos monsters are always female in all of these stories—into watery parts and solid parts, just like the irrigation ditches which the settlers in that part of the world gradually built up. The drainage and irrigation system divided the great slime of Southern Mesopotamia into dry land and flowing water. This is the great victory upon which life in that part of Mesopotamia comes to be founded. Since the Mesopotamians did not consider any other part of the world as worth bothering with, they simply made that victory the one in which the world comes to exist. The model is based on the experience of threatened chaos (which is a real threat), and then divine rescue from it. God or the gods battle disorder, dysfunction, and messiness, and that is why there is something rather than nothing.

The final and least profound of the non-Israelite creation models says that God or the gods merely *made* the world. This is a modern development, stemming from the eighteenth-century Enlightenment. It is perhaps best grasped from a famous analogy: when you see a watch you know there must have been a watchmaker, so when we see the much more complicated universe we think there must be a universe-Maker.

Such an idea of God is often called Deism—many of our founding fathers were deists if they had any religion at all. Franklin had none. Witherspoon is another question. Now mechanism either left no room at all for God or relegated him to the role of the original Engineer. If there is a God within the modern worldview, he is then the great Watchmaker, the one who made this elaborate mechanism in the first place according to his own wise design. But notice what that does not leave any room for. It does not leave any room for God's activity within this world. You see if God has to intervene to fix something, if the machine needs adjusting, that would only mean of course that he had been an imperfect Watchmaker in the first place. So the deist version of God is a God who set things up as a great mechanism and then spends the rest of eternity watching it work. Whatever the merits of the argument, watchmakers do not suffer with their cogs. At most, they intervene sometimes to set or clean or maybe repair them. On this view, then, there is no room for anything like the Lord of the Old Testament, like the Father of our Lord Jesus Christ.

Now notice that in all three of these cases—and they cover the waterfront of the world's religious faces—there is an antecedent condition. In the last two cases there is the chaos or there is in the final case whatever materials are lying to hand. Israel's doctrine can be boiled down into a denial of that antecedent condition. There is God and there is other reality, and the latter is sheerly because God chooses it shall be and that is the entire story. He does not make it out of anything. He does not emanate it from himself. He does not conquer something. It is just him and the result of his choice. That is it.

One may ask how Israel came to dissent from the general religious opinion. The reason is that it conceived the existence of the world as an act of the same God who called Moses and Abraham and so conceived the existence of the world as the same kind of event as the existence of Israel, which brings us to the first chapter of Genesis. Six times over, "And God said, 'Let there be . . .'" and it was. God, according to Genesis, calls the world into being as he called Israel into being when he spoke to Moses or to Abraham. It can also be said that the first chapter of Genesis incorporates the best science of its own day. The first chapter of Genesis is a late document in the collecting and writing of the Old Testament. It was created by exceedingly learned folk. Now their science is not as good as ours, but they got more right than you would think. The sequence of the six days is not so different from that posited by contemporary cosmology. You have an initial explosion of energy, and then a general sorting out of the cosmos, and then a general sorting out of the world within the cosmos, and then what can only be described as an evolutionary development of life forms. Moreover, besides incorporating the best science of its day, the explanation is conceptually very sophisticated. The Lord said let there be light and there is light and the Lord looks at the light and sees that it is good. Notice the progression. God just speaks the world into existence. The existence of the world is a response to a speech by the Lord. And the result of this exchange is an increase in value. That of course may not be a true account. We may be here for no reason whatsoever or we may be here on account of pansexuality.

But this at any rate is the answer to which Israel came at the peak of its own theological development.

What does God create? How does he do it? Both answers are given in Genesis: "In the beginning God created the heavens and the earth." Now the chaos that seems to appear here—"and the earth was without form and void, and darkness was upon the face of the deep"—is simply the first step in creation. And then we find that "In the beginning God created the heavens and the earth. . . . And God said, 'Let there be light'; and there was light. And God saw that the light was good. . . . And there was evening and there was morning, the first day." And so on. There has been an enormous amount of unnecessary worry about what "day" means here. And I think that the answer is that in the cosmology of the time with which Genesis operates, we do not have the slightest idea what it means. It meant a period of time and that is the end of the matter. So first there was a period of time in which "light" came. I suggested something like light came as a result of the big bang, the initial explosion of energy. Then there is a progressive sorting out. "And God said let the waters above the firmament be separated from the waters below the firmament. And God saw the firmament and said that it was very good. And there was evening and there was morning . . . and so forth." This happens six times over. It comes in two sections. First you get a kind of general sorting out of the universe and then you get days devoted to life. And that expresses a moral judgment: the universe is there for the sake of life. Then the life as it appears gets progressively more complicated. There is no theory given as to what causes the increasing complexity, nothing like the theories involved in Neo-Darwinism. It is just that God wanted it that way. He said "Let it be," and it is.

What sorts of creatures are there? There is no mention of them in Genesis but, as the story goes on, it becomes apparent that there are first of all angels. What is an angel? The Bible is full of stories about angels. None of them is altogether coherent with the rest. You are not going to get a definition of what constitutes an angel. So of course theologians have devoted a great deal of time to answering that unanswered question. Hildegard of Bingen furnishes us with a kind of inventory of angels which she takes from Dionysius the Areopagite's *Celestial Hierarchy.* It catalogues all the different kinds of angels that the Bible mentions. So there are archangels, regular angels, seraphim, cherubim, principalities, dominions, and powers and that makes seven.

The existence of a tempter (i.e., Satan, the Devil, Lucifer, the Old Serpent, etc.) is an ongoing conviction not just of Christianity but also of Judaism. And this reflects more than anything else a common experience: there does seem to be somebody out there laughing at us. I was very skeptical about the existence of Satan until I made that observation. The disasters that happen could just be disasters, but we seem to be mocked by them. And that is the main title of Satan throughout the tradition; he is the Mocker, the one out there laughing at us. I do not imagine many of you will have run into C. S. Lewis's *Screwtape Letters.* That is the best satanology of the modern period.

If everything that exists is created by God, how can there be a Satan? How can this earth be infected by a Mocker or a Tempter? There is nothing about that in the Bible. The standard understanding with which people have operated for centuries is not scriptural and it runs like this. Satan is a fallen angel. The very first angel created named Lucifer, which means "bearer of light," was so great and powerful and glorious and lit up that he finally could not stand that there should be anybody above him. That is to say, he could not stand that he was a creature. And in rejecting to be a creature, he fell into that which can only be described as nothingness. That is to say, there is nothing to Satan except his deficiency. All there is to Satan is what he is not. He does not really exist and yet there he is.

The last step is the creation of humanity. Now it is important to notice that this happens on the same day as all the other land animals. There is not a day devoted to us. I once heard a lecture by a noted professor from California of what at the time was called "deep ecology" who carried on for about a half an hour about the wickedness of the Christian faith because in our creation story an entire day was devoted to the creation of humanity. Well he had never read the story, obviously, because there is not an entire day devoted to the creation of humanity. There *is* a day devoted to the creation of the land animals—that is to say, so far as they were aware at the time, the most complex forms of life. So the one thing hammered home in the doctrine of creation with respect to us is that we are animals, complex ones, maybe the most complex in certain respects, but animals. We do not start off as spirits or souls; we start off as animated bodies, which is what "animal" means. There are unanimated bodies as well. There is, however, a break between the creation of the other land animals and the creation of humanity. God as it were pauses for a second of deliberation: "What shall we do next?" is in effect what it is about. "Let us make . . ." and then comes an interesting word. The natural way to translate it is "man." However, the word in Hebrew is a noun "*ha-adam*" which means earth. Let us make the one taken from earth. And following this deliberation which separates the human race from the other animals, two things then appear about *ha-adam,* "the Adam." You see this is both his name and his description, and it is not even "he" exactly. "Let us make man in our own image … male and female he created them." That is to say that this man created in God's image is somehow both a male and a female.

6 | The Image of God

Human beings are said to be the image of God. From the very first and throughout its history Christian theology has devoted a great deal of time and thought to trying to understand what this means. And indeed exegetes and theologians continue to dispute the matter today. Putting the question in metaphysical terms, what sort of being is specifically human being? Or to put the question in biblical terms, what is the specifically human relationship to the Lord? And if we suppose that there is something specific about the human relationship to the Lord, how do we go about living in accord with the fact that we are *this* sort of being, or that we have *that* particular and specific relationship to the Lord? What does it mean to be made in God's own image? Clearly the point is not that we *look* like God. We do not.

It has been suggested that being male or female is part of what is meant by the "image of God." The idea is that just as there is differentiation in God—Father, Son, and Holy Spirit—so there is differentiation in humanity. There are some big theological names attached to this proposal. Whether it is correct or not—I do not know. But it can be doubted.

Christian theologians very early adopted the language of "human nature" in response to this and many other questions. But what is a nature? The English word "nature" is a derivative of the Latin word "natura," which in turn was the standard translation of the Greek word "physis." So the question must be, "what is a *physis?*" Think of the matter this way. Suppose that "X is brown," that "X is vertebrate," that "X is two-stomached or ruminative," and continue assembling predicates like these until it becomes obvious that X is a cow. Notice, now, that some of the predicates just named could be stricken without X ceasing to be a cow. "X is brown" is one example. "X has a broken horn" could be stricken as well. Certain others could not. If X were not vertebrate, say, then it simply could not be a cow. An amoeba or a worm—yes. But not a cow. Now if we were to assemble all of the predicates that could not be stricken without ceasing to identify X as a cow, the sum of that mutually coherent complex of predicates would amount to the *physis, natura*, or *essential* of X.

In this respect all things (and not just animate things like amoebas and cows) have essences or natures. Rocks are inanimate, for example. Nevertheless, you could describe the essence of being a rock just by assembling all the predicates that something would need in order to be a rock. In any case, according to this conception "human nature" refers to the mutually coherent complex of characteristics that Jones or Alinsky or whoever must have in order to belong to the class "human being"—that is, to count as being made in "the image of God." What, then, does this mutually coherent complex of characteristics include? If to be the image of God is to possess a set of characteristics that are analogous to certain divine attributes, precisely what does that set include? Attempts by Christian theologians to answer this question have tended toward morally perilous exclusions. If, for example, we say that one of the essential characteristics of humanity is rationality—and everybody who has set out to define the image of God in this way has said this—then what of those in whom reason seems to be absent? What about those in the final stages of Alzheimer's or in permanently vegetative states? Are such persons not human, so that we may as well save our money and our grief by simply disposing of them? That is not an abstract invention of a problem. Quite the contrary, proposals that persons in permanently vegetative states are no longer human and therefore should be relieved of their burden are routinely reported in the newspapers.

Attempts to define the image of God in terms of "human nature" have regularly encountered a number of morally perilous difficulties. Just so, Christian theologians have regularly found themselves driven to bend and twist the concept of nature. One might say that in the Christian tradition the very notion of "natures" has been subjected to a kind of a subliminal, sub rosa critique. In modernity this critique finally leaked into the general discourse of the West. Indeed, this has gone so far that it has sometimes been said in late modern thought that there is no such thing as human nature, that each of us is simply what he or she determines himself to be by actions and decisions that make up life as we go along. You can see this radical critique of natures graphically presented in Jean-Paul Sartre's *Nausea,* in which the protagonist finally could not tell himself from a lobster. There is a narrator there but he has no firm grip on what it is he is narrating. Sartre's point is that there is no actual human nature, only a sort of story that I make up as I go along by the choices I make and the decisions I take. Here I simply am; I exist. And I exist as I live, as I act, as I choose, and that is the whole truth about me. Essence is some sort of a slime trail I leave behind as I wiggle my way through time.

And then you can proceed to the consequences of the notion that there can be no agreed upon standard of what humans are and should do. The actual denial that there is such a thing as human nature is sheer anarchy. If each of us effectively has a different nature from all of the rest of us, then we have no common basis for judgment and action. There is no such thing as a common morality.

And indeed, a notable aspect of late modern nihilism that is now regularly asserted (but never argued) is that human being is not different from, say, bovine being. This is usually adduced as a reason for treating cows with the same standards by which we regulate our relations to each other. But if we are to treat cows as we treat each other, that also means we can treat each other as we do cows. And that has already been tried in an immeasurably horrendous social experiment. The farmer who is concerned for the welfare of his herd will take certain measures. He will cull and breed the herd for what he takes to be advantages and virtues. This is not wicked; it is simply speeding up natural selection and organic evolution. The eugenics movement of the early twentieth century applied the same principles to the human population. The United States was one main center of that movement and another was Sweden. There were proposals to use birth control for purposes of natural selection. There were even attempts to sterilize those seen as unfit to pass on their genetic characteristics. But the big effort was made by the National Socialists in Germany. The Nazis were eugenicists. They believed that one strain, namely, the Aryan strain, was superior in the human population. The reason for getting rid of the Jews was that the Jewish population of Europe was taken to be a decidedly inferior strain who were rapidly contaminating the Aryan strain by intermarriage. This, they thought, had to be halted. And the simplest way to do that was simply to kill them. And that, finally, is what the Nazi eugenicists came up with. So that experiment has been made.

So on the one hand there are morally perilous consequences to uncritically conceiving the image of God in terms of "human nature." Certain human beings are inevitably excluded. But on the other hand the wholesale rejection of the notion of "human nature" leads to moral anarchy. In light of these problems it has to be asked which comes first in understanding *particular* human beings. Which comes first in understanding me? Is it more important that I am an instance of the class "human beings" because I possess a certain set of characteristics or dispositional properties in common with all the others in that set? Or is it more important that I am simply this person of whom it then may also be observed that I am in fact a human being. Which comes first in understanding *me*— that I am *this* human being or that I am *a* human being? That I am *this* person or that I am *a* person? When it comes to understanding *me,* should the accent fall on what we may call my "personal identity" or what we may call my "essential identity"?

In my view, Christian theology should give the first answer to each form of this question. It is my personal identity, first, and my essential identity or nature, second, that counts in understanding me. To understand me, you must first understand that I am *this* person and only then that I am an instance of the class "human beings." How, then, can we carry through a priority of the person to nature, of existence to essence, if you like? Of personal identity to natural identity or essential identity? How do we carry through that priority without giving license to moral anarchy?

We may begin by returning to Scripture. The book of Genesis and indeed Scripture as a whole does not define what it means to be the image of God by specifying a set of essential characteristics. Scripture does not speak in this way. No. It rather animates a history, a story, in which individuals and groups act in accord with their various places in that story, in that history. What Christian theology ought to say—and sometimes comes very close to saying—is that what you and I and Smith and Jones and Alinsky and so forth have in common is not in the first place an essence or nature. What we have in common is the story in which we appear—the drama in which each of us has a defining *role*. What is that role? It is to be the image of God. And that means, first, that human beings are peculiarly related to nature by which I mean here "all that stuff that is just there." On the one hand, Genesis says that we are land animals, created on the same day as the rest of the land animals. As such we are a part of all that stuff. Nevertheless, Genesis also says that we are involved, besides the relationship to our fellow animals, in a different set of relationships, those established by our being the image of God. Theology has used the word "freedom" as a slogan for this distinction between humankind and nature.

That distinction, by the way, comes from the Greeks. Freedom, for Aristotle, was rather limited in its scope. Women stayed home having babies and caring for them because they were thought to be a part of nature. Servants, too, were bound by nature insofar as they *had* to do whatever it was they were doing. Like women, they were thought to be bound by necessity like any other part of nature. The free man, by contrast, is the one who is free from nature in the sense that what he does he does not have to do, which in Aristotle's immediate political context, meant he is at liberty to attend to the business of the city, to be an office-holder, to vote and attend when the city assembly met, to serve in the army. All these are the proper doings of those who are not bound to nature. What Christianity did to this distinction was to say that on account of what we read about in Genesis, *all* humans are free. That is to say that human beings are not simply items in the natural processes as the Greeks had thought women and servants were.

To be free in this way is to be capable of being a kind of counterpart or conversation partner of God. This, in my view, is the heart of what is meant by the claim that human beings are made in the image of God. To be made in the image of God is to be something like God's "counterpart." What it means to be created in the image of God is that human beings are creatures with whom God can have an active exchange, a back and forth, a *relationship*.

The other thing that happens with humanity that does not happen with the animals is that God strikes up a conversation. Among the animals in the book of Genesis, the human animals are the ones that God talks to and who are expected to talk back. God strikes up a conversation with human beings. So it turns out that the counterpart relationship is effectively a discourse, a back and forth of address and response.

Notice, then, that the doctrine of the *imago dei* is just an extension of Israel's basic principle of religion. God talks to Abraham and Moses, and Moses and Abraham talk back. But now it is not just Moses or Abraham, and that is to say it is not just Israel; it is simply the human race as such. In the beginning it is the human race that is in conversation with God. This of course raises a question: precisely how is it that the God of

Israel talks to Moses? How is it that somehow God speaks to *us*? Many Jewish, Muslim, and Christian theologians would say that God speaks to us through the moral law. But there is a more fundamental answer still: you pray. It might be possible, then, to say that according to Genesis and so according to Jewish and Christian theological tradition, the human being is defined as the "praying animal." You will see this reflected throughout the history of the church from Augustine to Hildegard of Bingen to Barth. What do they constantly exhort you to do in the perilous journey through this life? Pray!

So to be made in the image of God is to have a role, and that role is to be in a relationship and a discourse with God and to occupy a place in the story that God has and lives with his people. And that story is not random, but has a plot. And the plot is given to it by the presence in the story of its author. What is really there within each of us, instead of what the Greeks call a *physis*, is rather something in which each of us participates—an ongoing drama with a plot. The human plot, the human story that is actually in progress, the play that is actually being produced, does have a plot and the plot is given to it by the presence of the author as also one of the dramatis personae. The story holds dramatically together and we do therefore indeed have something in common precisely because the author is triune, the triune God that I attempted to construe for you. In God, personal identity is indeed prior to essence. God the Father is first of all Father of that other personal identity the Son and he has that nature we call divine nature only in and by and on account of that relationship. The relationship and the personal identity given in the relationship—Father to the Son—*that* is the first fact about God. And that he is God—and then we will start laying out predicates: omnipotent, omnipresent, and so on—*that* is the second thing. So also then the Son: Jesus of Nazareth is first of all the Son of the Father and only thereby does he have the "divine nature." So also then the Spirit: the Spirit is first of all the mutual Spirit of the Father and the Son together and only by and in that relationship can he be construed as divine. In God the personal identities are constituted in each one's relationship to the other two.

And then, in that one of those three is one of us; our life together has a structure determined by the structure of the divine life. We have something in common by which we hold together, through which we can come together. We have that which in Greek thought was enabled by the notion of nature in that God is the God I tried to evoke for you earlier. So, I am who I am—and of course Popeye would say, "And that is all that I am, I am Popeye the sailor man!" And that is a drastic statement of personal identity—in and by my relational place in the history God has with us, and just and only so there is indeed something we may call human nature if we wrench that word from some, at least, of its original associations and make it mean something like the word I have been using, the "plot" of the human story.

7 | Sin and Salvation

Why should the death and resurrection of this one ancient Israelite be such a big deal? Suppose you even grant what has been claimed for him so far: that he personally sums up in his life and in his mission the history of God with God's chosen people Israel; that he is the coming king, the coming prophet, the Messiah on whom all Israel's hopes finally came to rest; that when he came it would finally be done. Suppose you even grant that Jesus was something like the *shekhinah* in person. What difference does that make in your and my situation?

You will have noticed that Christian theology treats some standard doctrinal topics. Thus far we have covered the doctrines of the Trinity and creation, and we have also discussed the *imago dei*. We now stand at the doorway of the doctrine that in Christian theology is usually called the doctrine of the atonement. The word "atonement" is a deliberate coinage, and a very old one that can be traced back to the sixteenth century—perhaps as early as 1516. It comprises three syllables—*at—one—ment*, each of which can be etymologically linked to the earlier noun, "onement" as well as the old phrase, "to be atone." So "atonement" means putting things that have been separated, but should not be, back together.

It is a supposition of Christian theology that our relationship to God is ruptured, that we are not at one with him and that we need to be. We have spoken of this rupture before. Earlier we saw how it was acted out in the history of Israel as the prophets interpreted it, but then in the story of creation we saw that, in fact, this rupture took place long before there even was an Israel. The legend of the fall of humankind says that "the Adam" turned aside from the creator, and that his disobedience precipitated a rupture, a relational breach that somehow continues to afflict all of humanity and separates us from God. This brings us to the unpopular subject of sin, which is a presupposition of the doctrine of the atonement.

What is sin? The first thing to be said is that it is not principally an ethical concept. Christian discourse about sin is not (or at least should not be) centered principally on lists of things that are good to do and things that are not. Sin is rather a *theological* concept—meaning, it refers first and foremost to something about the relationship between human beings and God. We can begin to grasp the content of that "something" by recalling how God creates. Earlier we said that God creates Israel by speaking to it— by calling Abraham, then Moses, and then—finally, at Mt. Sinai—by speaking the entire people into existence. We also said that God creates Israel in roughly the way that he creates anything whatsoever. God speaks things into existence. Just by saying, "let there be" he calls creatures into being. Now, what is so unique about human beings, we said, is that God creates them not only by speaking *about* them. He also speaks *to* "the Adam." Here, we need to be more precise about the moral content of what God says.

Even the most trivial speech has at least some moral content. We get told at the checkout counter in the grocery store to "Have a good one." It is a perfectly trivial comment, but it nonetheless evokes a uniquely American (and a very thin) moral vision of what it would mean to have a good day, a good evening, a good hour, and so forth. So as I said, even the most trivial speech has at least some moral content. Now, in the creation story God's creative speech overflows with moral content. The Hebrew word "*tov*" is more or less equivalent to our term "for," and that is the word used in the divine pronouncements of creaturely goodness. For when God says, "Let there be fish" it is immediately then said that the fish thus created are *good*. Or, more accurately, it is immediately said that fish are something "good-for," which is to say that fish are good *for* something. The point is that fish serve some specific purpose of the one who calls them into existence.

This brings us back to Israel. When the Lord speaks Israel into existence at Mt. Sinai, he explicitly specifies the good that Israel is to live *for*. He specifies the good *life*, in other words, that Israel has been created to *live*. The moral content of the good life is elaborated in what is called "Ten Commandments." Now, the negative form in which most of those commandments are presented can be misleading. It is presumed, you see, that human beings by and large do not live as we should. But the point of the commandments is to direct human beings to the good life to which we are called. The life that is good for human creatures, the Lord tells Israel, is a life that honors the creator (rather than creatures posing as wanna-be gods.) It is moreover a life of religious observance, familial solidarity, sexual faithfulness, respect for life, legal responsibility, and generosity to others.

You can see from the way I have presented it that this account of the good life is not just for Israel but for humanity at large. Now if we consider these commandments, we will note that the good life that God proposes to human beings is not individualistically defined. It is rather *collectively* or *communally* defined. It follows that to affirm the will of God who creates us is to live in unity with God and with one another. You can sum up all of the Ten Commandments simply this way. In Israel's language, things like righteousness and justice mean mutual harmony, mutual faithfulness, coherence in society and in the family and in the faith enabled by God's guidance as provided fundamentally for Israel and for other societies in the Ten Commandments, God's law or *Torah*.

So what, then, is sin? Sin can be most simply defined as whatever breaks up this community. Specifically, it designates the fact that human beings reject our fellowship with God and, subsequently, with one another. And given that God is the creator, and since fellowship with God is the sole basis and purpose of our very existence, sin is nothing less than rebellion against what we *are*. Augustine gives a vivid picture of sin in the story he tells about his early years in college. "To Carthage then I came, where a cauldron of unholy loves bubbled about me." Augustine then goes on to make two specific points. First, those unholy loves were a kind of *illness*: he did not *really* love what he purported to love. Instead, what he really loved was being in love, which is to say, a certain state of his own being. And that means that in loving other things he was *really just* loving *himself*. This is the very definition of what Christian theology has called sin: it is that I take you, not for yourself, but as an occasion for my own experience of something or other. So that is what ailed him. He did not love; he loved to love.

"Sins" in the plural are whatever we do by way of rupturing our relationships with God and with each other. Thus, to pick up one of the commandments, for Christian thinking, greed is not evil because God disapproves of possessions as such but because greed undermines community. A greedy person is a menace to all around him. You will notice that this does not bode well for a society whose whole economic system is regulated by nothing but the self-restraint of the greedy.

Most Christian thinking—not all, but most—contends that we are, all of us, indeed captive to sin. The moral life abhors a vacuum. If we are not bound up together with God and one another, we will be bound up in our rebellion against him— whether consciously or unconsciously. Christianity, in other words, has drawn the conclusion that we are not at one with God or each other and, therefore, that we are bound up with death, bound up with our own destructive impulses. The point evokes what in Christian theology is usually called the doctrine of original sin.

There are two essential parts of the notion of original sin. The first comes from Augustine, who tells us that he formulated the doctrine by observing children. When was I an innocent baby? Never! A baby is simply a selfishness machine. (Now babies are cute and lovely, so we we will put up with their selfishness.) The point is that none of us can ever point to a time when we were *not* alienated from God. That is the sense in which sin is *original*. It means that there is no way to get back (chronologically or ontologically) to a time prior to our alienation from God. The second part of the doctrine is that it is true of everyone. Now how does this take place? How does it come about that the whole human race is captive to sin? Augustine suggested that, from the beginning, human beings have somehow been "catching sin" from each other.

Explanations of this transmission are multiple and various, and it needs to be said that there is no such thing as a universally accepted Christian doctrine of the transmission of original sin. Augustine connected it with the circumstances of birth: sexual intercourse takes us out of control of ourselves (and indeed it would not be any fun if it did not), so the very means by which human beings are generated is tainted by this loss of the mind's control of the body.

That is one theory. And if a radio preacher tells you about original sin, it will be something like this theory that he has in mind. I must say that I do not buy it. The greatest American theologian to date, Jonathan Edwards, gave a different explanation. He said: "I am evermore convinced that there is no limit to the ways in which persons can interpenetrate each other." If I am with a sinner, meaning simply another human being, and if I live among others like me, then just thereby I participate in their alienation from God just as they participate in mine. Edwards's understanding of original sin is also mine. The transmission of original sin seems to me to be more a matter of the social inter-connectedness of human existence. I am not defined by myself alone but also by my position in the whole history of the human race. And that history is a history of alienation from the creator and from one another. We overlap with each other; we are mutually implicated in everyone else's life. Of course, thinking about the matter this way does not solve all the problems—but it does strike me as more straightforwardly biblical.

Alienation, rupture of fellowship, refusal of community with God and each other—however you want to define it, we need atonement. How does that work? Earlier, I made it sound like there was something called *the* Christian doctrine of the atonement. Now I must be more specific. For it is a remarkable fact about Christian theology that there is no such thing as an official or even generally accepted doctrine of the atonement. This makes it a peculiar doctrine. Consider the doctrine of the Trinity: to reject it is simply to be something other than a Christian. By contrast (assuming, of course, you believe that human beings have been reunited with God), you can be a perfectly respectable Christian while rejecting any existing theoretical explanation for precisely how that works.

I want to give you a list of possible theories of the atonement. Notice, however, that the first possibility is not a theoretical explanation but rather a *story* that the other theories try to explain. The story that dominates the New Testament (it is not the only one in the New Testament, but it does dominate) is found in the book of Acts. Peter gives one of the first Christian sermons before a huge crowd of pilgrims at Jerusalem. Crucially, Peter says, "Let the house of Israel know that God has made him both Lord and Christ, this Jesus whom you have crucified" (Acts 2:36). He means that the same Jesus of Nazareth who proclaimed the immediacy of the kingdom, who identified its acceptance with acceptance of himself, who told and enacted parables of a kingdom where the dumb speak, the blind see, the deaf hear, the poor are made rich, and sinners are accepted, this Jesus—who was executed by the mob in Jerusalem and the Roman authorities—is the Christ who was promised to Israel; the church, then is the place where people live in the confidence that God's will will be done.

Peter's sermon captures the conviction of the first believers (and the continuing conviction of the church) that the whole story of the God of Israel reaches its climax in the crucifixion of Jesus of Nazareth. Now that climax (again in the conviction of the first believers and in the conviction of the church to this day) turns out to be the completion of humanity's rupture with God. Notoriously, Jesus uttered as he hung on the cross, "My God, my God, why have you forsaken me?" The rupture and alienation between humanity and God that we have just called "sin" achieves its *fulfillment* and *completion* in the death of Jesus. So the climax of God's story with Israel turns out to be the rupture with God and the death that it entails.

God raised Jesus from the dead. And it is in *this* event that the unity of God and humanity is restored on the other side of sin and death. It is a unity that incorporates sin and death within itself and thus transcends the crucifixion. Christ was crucified; in him sin and death have achieved their fulfillment. But Christ also lives. And he lives, moreover, *precisely as* the Christ of Israel so that the sin and death in which God's story with Israel climaxes is transcended because it is included in Christ's living existence. A new community is moreover established in the resurrection, and that community, the church, is a community that claims to know the crucified and risen Jesus as the Christ, the holy one of Israel who dwells among them in prayer and, perhaps above all, in the bread and cup in the fellowship meal, which is the central ceremony of the church's life. And this community is a *missionary community* that accepts all who believe in and are baptized in the name of the Father, the Son, and the Holy Spirit. It follows that others can share in the life of this risen Jesus. That he is crucified and risen is also true of those initiated into and sustained within this new community. So Paul says in the sixth chapter of Romans that we have already died with Christ and we look forward to being resurrected as he was. There is in the life of the church (at least, so it is claimed) a sharing in the resurrected life of Christ wherein sin and death are transcended.

Thus far the New Testament's predominant story is of the death and resurrection of this one Jew. You have to remember that this story is simply told as the climax of the whole story of the Old Testament. The difference that story is meant to make in our lives is understood as the difference that the *denouement* and *peripeteia* of that story make for the participants in it.

The missionary movement of the church out of Galilee and Jerusalem and into the Mediterranean world was a movement into the Roman Empire and the educational system structured around the great thinkers of ancient Greece. If you went to school in AD 50 anywhere in the Roman Empire, what you learned was fragments of Plato and Aristotle, a few fragments of the Greek rhetoricians, as well as Roman law. This movement into the Roman Empire brought people into the church who had their own antecedent ideas about death and the possible rupture of our relationship with God, and what might be done about that. At least many of these people had little to no acquaintance with the Old Testament. So once again, just as with the doctrine of the Trinity, it happened that while converts were perfectly willing to acknowledge that Jesus's death and resurrection had made a difference in their lives, they nevertheless required new explanations of the New Testament story. Those explanations required not just a story, but also theoretical accounts of how the death and resurrection of this one man could make a universal difference.

In the course of theological history, several theories have been propounded. They are not mutually coherent. Still, each of them is valuable in its own terms, though none is universally accepted. I am going to spend some time acquainting you with a typology of theories about why the death and resurrection of Jesus make a universal difference. There is a book by a Swedish theologian of the last generation, Gustav Aulen, called *Christus Victor*. I am going to follow it roughly here, though not without a number of critical revisions and at least one addition. We will sort these out historically, among very broadly defined periods in which they have been successively dominant.

The first is the many centuries of the church's life when the culture and polities of Roman Mediterranean antiquity were more or less still there. This ended in the seventh century, when Islamic jihad conquered the African and Middle Eastern heart of the ancient church and cut the sea routes between the Eastern and Western churches.

The church's intellectual and spiritual leaders during this long period are customarily referred to as the "Church Fathers," for their formative role in shaping the church's subsequent life. (None of them are called "Church Mothers" since they were all male—an undoubtedly unfortunate fact, but a fact nonetheless.) Most of them were in the eastern half of the church, which has tended to be the home of theories and thinkers. The Church Fathers tended to be extraordinarily well educated. They tended to know the great pre-Christian Greek thinkers inside and out, and they tended to know the Bible inside and out. They by and large worked with two themes in describing the atoning power of the death and resurrection of Christ, which they sort of mixed and matched as the occasion required.

You will find an exemplary instance of the first theme, dei-
fication, in Athanasius of Alexandria's *On the Incarnation.* So,
when he tells us that "God became man in order that man should
become God," he means the lost unity of God and humanity has
been restored in the personal constitution of this one person,
Jesus, and that his death and resurrection opened this restoration to others.

The second is cosmic conflict. On this view, history as told by
Scripture is understood as a history of conflict between God and
cosmic powers opposed to him. There is a fair bit of what moderns would call mythology in this construction. It says that there
is more in heaven and earth than your philosophy could ever
imagine. There are demons and there are big demons like Satan.
And there is death, which is not just something that happens to
people but rather a force operating in the world. And there is
sin, which is not just a human failing but is again a kind of force
operating in the world. And the whole history of humankind
narrated paradigmatically in the scriptures is a history of warfare between God and these anti-God powers.

Putting it crudely, the death of Christ is conceived of as the
great strategic stroke of God in this conflict and the resurrection is the success of that stroke. Thus, the atoning power of the
death and resurrection of Christ is that of the final triumph in
the battle between God and Satan (that figure out there laughing
at us that I talked about earlier)—a battle that constitutes the
plot of all history.

It should not be too hard to see the value of this construction.
It is not difficult to read the history of the human race as a history of warfare between good and evil. And if we suppose there is
a God, we can also understand our history as a history between

God and evil. That, in fact, makes a great deal of empirical sense. Then, too, if you read the story as the Bible does, then this worst thing that ever happened—the crucifixion of the Messiah, the Christ—and the triumph over that worst thing—the resurrection of Christ—can be construed as the final or at least the decisive victory in the warfare between God and evil.

We move to the medieval period. A man named Anselm who was Archbishop of Canterbury in the twelfth century produced what became a sort of standard Western doctrine of atonement and remains in a way standard to this day. Anselm said that the moral structure of the universe is something like (and this is only an analogy) a perfect feudal system. The morality of the feudal system of the Middle Ages had as its central concept the notion of honor. You fulfill your place in society by showing honor to those for whom honor is due and by receiving honor from those who owe you. Today, we still have a faded version of that intuition: some people do deserve our honor and we are remiss if we do not give it.

On this view, the all-important and simplest rupture of fellowship between God and us is constituted in that we do not honor God *as* God. If God is God, then he is the only god and there is therefore nothing else at all in the universe that should be more important to us than him. Yet, we worship other things. We do not pray. We spend our days honoring our careers, success, and security. That the human race does not honor God, that we do not obey the first commandment, "You shall have no other gods before me," is not just a moral fault on the part of individuals; it is a disruption of the moral order of the universe upon which the well-being of the human race and indeed of God's creatures generally rests.

This, as Anselm tells the tale, poses God with a choice: he can let the human race go and start over again or decide that creatures are too much trouble to bother with and he can get along without them, or he can do something to restore the moral order, at least in one person. Christ's death on the cross therefore is the final act of obedience and honor by a human creature to God: obedience even unto death, honor even unto death. And the resurrection is God's acknowledgment that this has been done. Why should that do the rest of us any good? Because it is not just a man who dies on the cross, but it is the Son, the second person of the Trinity. So this death by a creature has the inner potency to reestablish the moral order generally.

Anselm himself tends to put this in feudal terms. The feudal arrangement viewed honor quantitatively. If I rebel against my immediate overlord—I am a man of arms and I do not grab my spear and my sword and shield and march out when the lord of the manner summons me—that is a minor violation of honor, and I can restore myself in proper accord with honor by doing something extra the next time or, as money came into circulation, via payment. If I do it against the duke, a greater repayment is necessary. If I do it against the king, a real whopping one is necessary. What if I do it against God? That requires an infinite payment because God is the infinitely valuable overlord whom I have dishonored. All the worth of the human race cannot pay off that debt. But Christ can because he is not just a man and therefore able to die, but also the second person of the Trinity and of infinite value in himself. Anselm's theory can be detached from the feudal system, and it has been. The theory does not have to work quantitatively, as it did for Anselm, so that the death and resurrection of Christ can be seen simply as the reestablishing of the moral order of the universe. In any case, his theory has been very influential even though there has always been a succession of theologians who have critiqued it severely. And of course you can guess where the critique will bite. The theory makes God look like a stuffy old feudal lord who is concerned about his own honor. Moreover, if you read the New Testament carefully you will discover that it nowhere speaks of our satisfying God. It is not God who needs to be pacified; it is us. So Anselm's theory is by its critics said to run the wrong way.

The most famous of those critics is the first one to have appeared and he may be the only one on this list of figures of whom maybe you all have heard: Abelard. He said Anselm has it backward. It is indeed not God who needs to be pacified; it is us. And what the death of Christ does according to Abelard is to act out, to make visible, the love of God for humanity. John 3:16, the one verse that everybody knows: "God so loved the world that he gave his only son." The death of Christ so acts out God's love for humanity that if we once see the cross, we cannot help but love God in return. Such theories are called "moral influence theories," and ever since Abelard they have come one after another, but they all have the same structure. What happens with the crucifixion and resurrection of Christ is an act on God's part to move us to abandon our rebellion or, to put it another way, to attract us to himself. The God hanging on the cross, says Abelard, is an attractive God, not a fearsome one. And being attracted to him is the atoning effect of the crucifixion.

At the outset I mentioned that each of these theories has its own merits when taken on its own terms. But I want to leave you with what, I think, is a more plausible theory that more nearly approximates the drama that (we have seen) climaxes in the New

Testament. One way to spell that theory out is by drawing on two figures and a term that I have not yet mentioned. The figures are Martin Luther and Hans Urs von Balthasar and the term is "justification," which simply means "to make just." Justification is whatever happens to make those who are unjust be just. In scripture and in most of the theological traditions, "to be just" is the same as "to be right." So there is another word you can use instead of "justice"—namely, "righteousness." Both mean "to be rightly related to God and your neighbor"—that is, to love the Lord your God with all your heart and with all your soul and with all your might, and love your neighbor as yourself. Thus, justification is either simply the same thing as atonement or (depending on your conceptual distinctions) an essential aspect of atonement. Here, I want to say that to ask, "How does God make us right with him" is just to ask, "How does God restore or "at-one" the community ruptured by sin?

In *Mysterium Paschale,* von Balthasar said that to be faithful to Scripture's record of the crucifixion and what immediately follows it, we must say that something *cataclysmic* and *intensely dramatic* happened between Jesus the Son and his Father. Jesus's cry on the cross, "My God, my God, why has thou forsaken me?" says von Balthasar, suggests that Christ was indeed forsaken by God the Father. It follows that in the life of God himself, there was an event in the style of *King Lear* or *Oedipus Rex,* where the story comes to a halt and it is unclear that it will resume. This is drama at its most intense. How does this event, this dramatic stop in God's own life, bring about atonement? In the *Theodramatik,* von Balthasar puts the point in terms of goodness and freedom. That God is good and that we *can* be good (these are von Balthasar's starting points in *Theodramatik*) means that, together, we and God can act freely. For von Balthasar (and surely he is correct), freedom occurs only in the meeting of *persons*. It is only when I meet someone different from me, and only if in that meeting I am *challenged*, that I might possibly become someone different from the person I already am. Freedom is a possibility for me, but it is not something that I possess; it is something that *occurs* in the meeting of one person and another. Specifically, it occurs when at least two persons pose new possibilities to one another—which is to say it only occurs in the context of a *drama*. Now, this is true of both God and man. Yet, God is free in himself because, as triune, he is a drama in himself—the *peripeteia* of which is Jesus's crucifixion. We, not being triune, are freed from sin and made one with God as we come to be involved in God's drama by participating in the life, crucifixion, and the resurrection of the Son. But how do we get involved in this drama? What does it mean to participate in the life, crucifixion, and resurrection of the Son? This brings me to Luther, who said that what unites us with God is not anything we do. It is not any of our "works." Rather, what unites us with God is "faith," which is nothing but our trust in what happens *in* Christ. It is precisely this faith and only this faith, this trust, that attaches our lives *to* the divine drama, which is a drama that God lives *for us*. That, I think, is how the death and resurrection of Jesus comes to make a difference in our lives.

8 | Church

At the beginning of this set of lectures, I said that the church was the community with a message: the gospel, the good news of Jesus's resurrection. At that point I simply wanted to say what theology is—namely, the thinking that this community gathered around this message must do in order to speak this message again. I also said that one could understand the relationship between the church and its message, the gospel, in two ways. One could say that the gospel is there to create this special community in the world called "the church." Or one could say that the church is simply the means to carry the gospel to the world. That is what we have in front of us so far about the church. Now it is time to take a look at the church for itself and a bit more deeply.

Theological reflection about the church is in many ways a modern development. For most of history, Christian theologians simply took the church as a presupposition rather than as something specific to be talked about. It was the fragmentation in the Western Church at the time of the Reformation that sparked the church's reflection on what it means to be the church. Yet, so long as each separate communion after the Reformations—the Reformed Church, the Roman Catholic Church, the Lutheran Church, and so forth—regarded itself as *the* church and the others as non-churches, each community felt no special, urgent problem about what it meant to be the church. But during the second half of the twentieth century, that is to say post–World War II, this bland conviction became, for a variety of reasons, hard to sustain. It was the so-called ecumenical movement that blossomed after the Second World War, roughly describable as the attempt to bring the fibers back together again, that brought the doctrine of the church or "ecclesiology" to the fore. For when my group (the church to which I belong) says of some group very different from my group (say, the church to which you belong) that it is also in some degree "church" (maybe not *the* church, but church nonetheless), the following question immediately becomes urgent. What is the church? Precisely what is this thing to which my group and your group and those other groups all more or less belong? What is *the* church like? How do we recognize it when we see it—assuming, of course, it even exists?

There are many ways to approach this question. Here I will take the one that provides the easiest outline. Despite the premodern church's relative disinterest in ecclesiology, the ancient church did bequeath us a standard list of the church's essential characters, which will do very nicely for a synopsis. The Nicene Creed—which is to say, the creed recited in the main services of most Christian groups— says that the church is "one, holy, catholic, and apostolic." I want to answer our question by speaking about each of these in turn.

First, the church is one. This carries a double sense. On the one hand, it means that there is literally one thing called the church, so that if two groups claim to be *the* church, and if one of them in fact is, then the other is not. As Paul said when bawling out the church he had founded in Corinth, "Is Christ divided?

So how do you go about being divided?" His point was that the church is one in the simple sense that there is only one of it. But then there is a second sense that refers to the the internal unity of the church with respect to its purpose. Passage after passage in the New Testament—most notably, Jesus's farewell prayer in the seventeenth chapter of John—says that the entire purpose of the gospel is to bring people into unity with God and so also with each other.

The word "church" is the word we use to translate a Greek word *ekklesia,* which roughly means gathering, assembly, or congregation. And at the very first there was one church in the simplest possible sense, namely, that there was just one congregation, in Jerusalem. It was led by at least some of the twelve apostles and, apparently, by James, who was the brother of Jesus. This group of Jews went to the temple to pray like all other Jews in Jerusalem did. And then they met by themselves for a special meal of bread and wine. But there were of course other followers of Jesus whom he had left behind elsewhere in his wanderings, particularly in Galilee. Moreover, persecution by the temple authorities drove many Christians out of the Jerusalem congregation. So very early there were plural gatherings of this one gathering and that immediately poses a problem that has been an occasion of debate ever since. If the oneness of the church does not reside in the fact that all Christians should be assembled as one group, wherein does it reside?

The answer turns on a related phenomenon: the church's mission spread quickly all over the Mediterranean and the Aramaic-speaking worlds. Christian missionaries went mostly to the cities. Hence, Paul's letters were all addressed to congregations in ancient cities (e.g., Corinth, Ephesus). But the message was soon carried to suburban and country constituencies. On account of this rapid expansion, the oneness of the church came to be understood in terms of mutual admission to the Lord's supper and mutual exchange of members and clergy. So that if I move from Corinth to Athens, I can be a member of the church at Athens. And such movement gradually became regulated by fellowship agreements between the pastors of those town churches, called "bishops." So if I move from Athens to Corinth, I bring you a letter from my pastor in Corinth saying, "Jenson was a tolerable member of our church. I would not call him outstanding, but a tolerable member. You ought to accept him in Athens as well."

Then in the fourth century, with Constantine (about whom we have talked before), the empire becomes overwhelmingly Christian. The territories led by some at least of the bishops became immense, having hundreds of thousands of members. This sprawling movement spread over the Mediterranean world very quickly, going into southern Europe and then east into the Aramaic-speaking territories that we now think of as Iraq, Iran, and the like. Over time, these communities grew apart in all manner of practices so that finally, in the eleventh century it was acknowledged that eastern and western churches were out of communion.

Nobody wanted to say that it was permanent. There were constant efforts to restore communion. And then, of course, there is the Western schism at the Reformation. The uproar of the Reformation resulted very quickly in territorial/confessional churches, which, despite their efforts to maintain fellowship, acknowledged that they too were out of communion. And then emigration from Europe and missionary activities in the

European churches spread those divisions all over the globe. So not only were the Church of England, let's say, and the Reformed Church of the Netherlands in dubious fellowship with each other, but their daughter churches in Africa were also out of fellowship with each other. And then, of course, you get the United States, in which the Protestant churches have been liable to division since their inception. So what about the *one* church?

Let me say something more about the ecumenical movement after the Second World War. Postwar reconstruction was handled largely by the churches; it was heavily financed by the government, of course, but mostly staffed by the churches. So there was an entire generation of church leaders who, as young people, had been working in refugee camps together across confessional lines. The possibility of working together as Christians posesd the question anew: "Why are we divided?" And as soon as that question was posed, one thing became obvious: if the church is one, then a divided church is dubiously a church at all. On all hands, therefore, an enormous effort of intellectual labor was put forth to see what could be done about at least reducing ecclesial divisions if not overcoming them altogether. In 1965, that was jump-started by a great council of the Roman Catholic Church, the so-called Second Vatican Council, which affirmed the ecumenical movement as an obligation also of the Roman Catholic Communion. Now since the Roman Catholic Communion was two thirds of all Christians, their entry into the movement gave it an enormous amount of momentum. Indeed, it can be said that the Roman Catholic Church now takes more responsibility for the ecumenical movement than the Protestant churches any longer do.

There have been two vehicles of that ecumenical movement. The one is so-called conciliar ecumenism, where representatives of all or some or many of the churches get together and produce documents, some of which go right to the shelf and are never read again, and some of which have become very important. (If you are at all interested you should look at the so-called BEM Report [Baptism, Eucharist, and Ministry] of the World Council of Churches.) The other is the so-called bilateral dialogues. These are teams set up by two churches not in fellowship with each other, with representatives from each side meeting two or three times a year for an indefinite period of years, working chip by chip on the matters taken to create the distance between those two churches. And there has been every conceivable kind of such dialogue. You name two churches and there is bound to have been a dialogue between them sometime or another. They take place at a world level, at a regional level, at a national level, and there are some successful dialogues that have taken place at a local level.

The church is holy. The notion of holiness is universal in the religious world. If you have had any comparative anthropology courses you have encountered the Polynesian notion of taboo, which in so much of the world is an equivalent of the Western and Jewish notion of the holy. The Hebrew word is *qadosh*. Now what does it mean to be *qadosh* or taboo? The holy is that which is radically different from everything else.

There is a great book by a German scholar Rudolf Otto called *The Idea of the Holy*. In summary, Otto's book says, "The holy is the *mysterium tremendum*," the tremendous mystery. The holy is the character of something that simultaneously so fascinates that we cannot get away from it and yet threatens to destroy us. It is a mystery—it fascinates, it draws, we cannot get hold of it, and for precisely that reason we keep trying to, and it is terrible. Augustine's description of what happened when he attempted the Neoplatonic ascent—when he saw this great light and felt it would shrivel him like a spider if he stared at it any longer—is a classical description of the holy.

Now the church is supposed to be holy. It is clear that if there is God, God is the supreme instance of the holy. Or rather, the other way around, holiness is his chief characteristic. Precisely because God is holy, the church claims also to be holy. Now what is the connection between the holiness of God and the holiness of the church? One way into that gives me the opportunity to pick up two main themes of contemporary ecclesiology. I said there was a big interest through the whole second half of the last century that is still going on in ecclesiology. Two main themes of the contemporary ecclesiology are a way to get hold of the holiness of the church—the connection of the church to the holy God.

One theme is that the church is the people of God. This picks up on the Old Testament idea of Israel as God's people. The church does not necessarily claim to be *the* people of God in the sense that the Jews are not, but it does claim to be the people of God. And that means that the church has to be so characterized as to be able to live with the holy God, to run with him. The church has to be and sometimes is radically different from everything else. Wherever you find the church attempting to woo the culture around it to recruit members by being as much like the world around it as possible, you will know that the church has become *un*holy. The church when it is the church is different. It is different ethically. You can count on it that whatever is taken to be really acceptable behavior in the world at any given time, the church will disapprove. Or at least it should.

The church is holy because it is the people of the holy God. That is the first theme. The second is that the church is holy insofar as it is the "body of Christ." We have already touched on the notion of the "body" as a theological category, but now we must work more systematically. Were it not for two sets of passages in the New Testament the notion of body would not be a specifically theological category. The one set of passages is the institution passages of the Lord's Supper: "The Lord on the night in which he was betrayed"—and I am reciting from the liturgy of my own denomination—"took bread and when we had given thanks, he broke and gave it to them saying, 'Take, eat, this is my body given for you.'" The other is the passage from chapters 10 and 11 in Paul's first letter to the congregation at Corinth. Corinth was a congregation that Paul had started and, as I hope I made you aware at some point, Paul continued to regard himself as the pastor of all the congregations he had started. Well, he could not be present to all of them simultaneously so he did a lot of his pastoral work by mail. No one knows how many letters Paul may have written. The ones that we have are the ones congregations, having gotten them, saved and then tended to swap with each other. "Well, we have a letter from Paul," said the people from Corinth. "Well, we have one too," said the people from Galatia, "Let's swap so we will both have both of them."

The congregation in Corinth was (like American Protestants) given to divisions and labels. They tended to label themselves and even got into a dispute about whether it was better to be one of Apollos's disciples or one of Paul's own disciples or somebody else's disciple. Paul regarded this divisiveness of the Corinthian congregation an offense against the very nature of the church. So he wrote the letter to Corinth—at least the first of them— as an attempt to combat the quarrelsomeness of the Corinthian congregation.

One of the occasions of their quarrelsomeness was that the rich would bring extravagant food to the community meal, which they refused to share with the poor. Now Paul wants to rebuke them, and this is how he does it. In one passage he says, "Because we all eat of the one bread, one loaf, we are one body." What does he here mean by "body"? That is what we are coming to. The other passage is more complicated: it insists that by violating your fellowship with each other, you are violating the oneness of that body which we are together because we eat the one loaf. And that body is the body of Christ. Therefore, your behavior at the Lord's Supper is blasphemy of Christ. And the body of Christ you are violating is the bread and wine on the table! That is to say, somehow or other, the loaf and the cup and the gathered congregation *are* the same body of Christ. Now how is that possible?

It is possible to take the term "body" there as a metaphor or an image. We do not have to take it with full seriousness and ask questions like "How can the same body be the congregation and the Lord?" Undoubtedly, most Protestants take it that way. Nevertheless, I think that is not linguistically correct. The way to check what Paul means by body, how he is using the term, is, of course, to look through the whole of his writings and see how the word "body" is used elsewhere. He uses it quite regularly of himself and he uses it in the context of where he wants to be with his congregation and cannot be, when he is distant. For example, he says, "I am sorry I am not there in the body, but I can write you this letter anyway. . ."

That has led me to propose the following sense for what Paul means by "body" (again, I mentioned this earlier, but now let us put it more exclusively): by "body," Paul means simply the person himself. It is Paul who is absent, who is not in Corinth, and who has to write a letter.

Suppose I were lecturing along and were disembodied, so that Jenson's soul is here but his body has gone away. It is conceivable that some kind of telepathic transmission could still take place. Maybe you would hear me talking in your head. But, if I offended you so that you wanted to rise up and heave me out the window, you would not know where to find me. Or if I so pleased you that you really wanted to get up and grab my hand and say, "Jenson, that was a marvelous lecture," you would not know where to find me. That is to say, the body of a person is the person himself or herself, insofar as that person is available to other persons. To say then that the church is the body of Christ is to say that here is manifestly a body, a corporate entity, and that entity is Christ as Christ is in the world and therefore available in the world. If the world wants to get rid of Christ, what it has to do is persecute the church because that is the place where Christ is available. If the world wants to hear Christ, all it has to do is listen to the church, because again that is the thing as which he is to be found. Similarly, within the church if the church wants to locate Christ, the place where he can be found, where he can be located, is the bread and cup on the table or on the altar. And these are the same body in both cases because there is only one Christ—the body *being* the person as available.

Third on the creedal list of characteristics of the church, the church is catholic. I think I had better make a preliminary set of remarks about the current use of the term "catholic." In the creed itself—"We believe in one, holy, *catholic*, and apostolic Church"—the word is an adjective applied to the one church wherever that is to be found.

But in much popular and semi-scholarly discourse the word "catholic" designates a certain attitude toward the traditions of the church. So, within one Christian denomination in the United States—the Episcopal Church—you can walk into one church and find the clergy dressed in vestments that reach back to the fourth century, and the music will be Gregorian chant. You can walk into another Episcopal church and very well find an overhead projection with little bouncing balls that teach you the place in a praise song. There, the main thing will be singing and preaching, and the pastor may be very well dressed in a T-shirt. Now in the popular, colloquial sense, the first of these churches is sometimes called "catholic" whereas the other is not. That same difference runs through the Lutheran Church, the Methodist Church, the Presbyterian Church, it evens runs through the American Catholic Church, though you will have a difficult time getting Catholics to admit that.

I mention this use of the word "catholic" only to set it aside. When we call the church "catholic" and we are using the word in a more than a colloquial sense, what are we saying? There is a double reference. On the one hand, we are saying that the church makes a coherent whole in itself—to use language that is popular these days, both synchronically and diachronically, that is to say, both in its extension at any one time and across its whole history. There is a community that is extended both temporally and spatially and it makes a coherent whole both in its teachings and its practices.

You can almost use the word "culture" at this point. Ethnographers use the word "culture" for a community and all of the language and practices which hold that community together, which make it a community across time and across space. The church has its own culture and the church is faithful to itself then when it sticks to that culture.

In the second sense, the church is supposed to be a church that embraces humankind. You may not like this. This may be offensive: the church absorbs and transforms the cultures to which it comes. The first instance of that was the move out of Jerusalem and Judea into places like Athens. No sooner were there Christians in Athens than the leaders themselves were philosophers and started mining Aristotle for what they could find in him. The same happened with music and art in the fourth century shortly after Constantine. Where did Christian sculptors learn how to sculpt? From pagan sculptors. Yet the whole feel of Christian sculpture is decidedly different. The pagan statuary is there to be looked at. The figures pay no attention to you looking at them. They are being beautiful in order to be stared at. The figures of Christian sculpture, on the other hand, are staring back at you. The Christian movement at the beginning had no sculpture. In fact, Christians were a little bit dubious of sculpture because of the commandment "thou shalt not make a graven image," but they absorbed the culture and did their own thing with it. And that, by the way, is how all cultures go about it. It is by stealing from their neighbors.

Finally, the church is "apostolic." The word "apostle" means someone sent on a mission. "The" apostles are those first sent out to speak the gospel beyond the initial followers of Jesus. There will be two qualifications for that. To be an apostle in this initial sense, one will have to know who Jesus is and will have to be able to witness firsthand to the message, that is, Jesus is risen. The Gospels contain references to an inner circle of Jesus's disciples, the "twelve" apostles whom Jesus sent out on preaching and healing missions even before his crucifixion. These same twelve seem to have been the chief initial missionaries. But there are others than the twelve who were remembered in that role, most notably Paul who was not one of the twelve apostles but who became the most wide-ranging missionary of them all.

What then does it mean for the church to be "apostolic," turning the word "apostle" into an adjective that applies to itself? From one point of view, this is simply the registration of a fact: the church starts with those apostles. But the claim of apostolicity is the claim that the church is now faithful to that beginning, that the gospel it proclaims is the same as the gospel of those apostles, and that the culture that is interior to it is somehow continuous with the culture of the church as it was. And here, how do you describe that continuity? What is constituent of it? Here there is again disagreement. There is general agreement that one constituent is agreement in the message to be brought. The church is apostolic in that it is faithful—it hopes—to the initial proclamation "Christ is risen." There is somewhat less agreement that the apostolicity of the church is constituted by the continuity of tradition back to the apostles in a more comprehensive sense, to include not just a teaching of the gospel but also the intellectual tradition that has grown up around the teaching of the gospel, the liturgical tradition, and so forth. But where the spirits divide is at this point: is the apostolicity of the church constituted also by the succession in office from those initial apostles? That is to say, did Paul and others of the initial twelve (and however

many others there were) in some sense form a group holding
a joint office, to which others then can succeed? This is sometimes called the "historic episcopate," meaning the succession of
apostolates who are now called now "bishops." Take the case of
Peter; it is claimed that he was the bishop of Rome. Is that right?
And if so did he have a successor? Has there been a succession
of bishops in Rome? And if there has been a succession, is this
important to the apostolicity of the church now in Rome? The
Roman Catholic Church, the Orthodox churches, the Anglican
Communion, and the Lutheran churches of Sweden and Finland
say that the succession of bishops in office is constitutive of the
church's apostolicity. Most Protestant groups do not.

To understand the issue, you have to of course know what
a bishop is. The word means "overseer." Early Christianity was
an urban phenomenon as I mentioned earlier. So there was a
congregation of Christians in, for example, the city of Corinth,
but Christians in the suburbs and countryside were also
attached. By at least 150, no later than that, some congregations
like that were led by a single head pastor called the bishop,
the overseer of the congregation. By 200, nearly all Christian
congregations had that structure. Then, as Christianity took
over the empire, congregations arose of course in the suburbs and the countryside with their own leaders, but they
were still supervised by the town bishop, which produces
what is called the "diocese," the territory of which the bishop
is the head pastor. That general structure persisted to the
Reformation, when most German bishops refused to ordain
graduates of Wittenberg—that is, persons tainted by association with Martin Luther. For the followers of the Reformation,
that refusal cast the authority of the bishops themselves into

question. Regional churches of the Reformation—not all of them—and left-wing movements emerged and got along without bishops in the old style and without the historic succession. So the new bishop of Oslo, and he was still called bishop, was, however, not consecrated by the old bishop of Oslo. So the historic episcopate, the historic succession was broken. And most Protestant bodies in this country still get along—or they at least think they get along—without bishops in the historic succession. By and large, in the ecumenical movement the historic episcopate seems to be winning out in the argument, but that is a separate matter.

9 | Can These Bones Live?

W e must now confront the possibility that what we have been talking about is a pile of dead bones. To introduce that subject I am going to go back to the Emperor Constantine. When Constantine in the fourth century not only made Christianity legal, but made it the at least semi-official religion of the empire, he created a situation which was drastically new for the church. The church had lived for three hundred years in hiding. Now, to be a Christian was suddenly in vogue. Of course, that did not mean that the old imperial cults, and the mystery religions, and so forth, just went away. It did mean that to be a Christian very quickly conferred a cultural and social advantage. Let me give you an impression of the new social arrangements and structures that the church had to create to confront its new circumstances.

The church had thus far maintained a strict discipline among its members, and it could do that without harshness or bureaucracy. The bishops and other clergy of those tight little congregations—living closely together per force since the rest of society would not accept them—knew the members, and the members knew each other. So persons who were living in a way inappropriate to a believer would be found out. The bishop would call them in for a little chat. If they confessed to what they had been doing, they would be admitted to penance. That is to say, they would be excluded from participation in the Lord's Supper for a period of time, which could vary from weeks to years depending on what they had been up to. During this time they were also expected to fast in particular ways and devote themselves to works of charity. And if they held out through their time of penance, they would then be permitted to confess their sins to the whole congregation—which in my case would be easily the worst part of the whole thing. I am Norwegian, and we do not open up. After this confession, they would again be allowed to receive the bread and wine.

A single bishop at first could handle all of that on his own. But what was he to do now with thousands of new congregants? What would he do when he was expected to deal with, let's say, fifty blatant fornicators and a couple of false monks? What happened was what had to happen. The church created a system of rules and regulations—so many days of penance for such and such sin. But even this system was quickly overwhelmed by the sheer bulk of penitents. Church discipline thus became a far less beneficent and communal affair and rather more like the Internal Revenue Service. That is just one aspect of the change effected by what we may call the "Constantinian Settlement."

For some, like John Howard Yoder and Stanley Hauerwas, this phrase designates something analogous to the fall of humankind. Roman Catholic theologians, on the other hand, often speak of the church's establishment as a glorious providence and disposition of God, on account of the certainly many good things that came of it. I mean to suggest neither of those things here. The important point is that for better or worse, the church's gradual and inevitable interaction with the ideals, laws, and culture of Greco-Roman civilization eventually produced what can only be called a Christian civilization. It endured in Europe, the Americas, and to some extent in territories colonized by Europe until just a few years ago. I would like to take a look at a few aspects of what this civilization was like.

We have already noted on several occasions that educated believers in the centuries after Constantine were steeped in the texts of Plato and Aristotle and in the texts of later thinkers like Plotinus. Then, too, we said they were educated in the texts of Greek physicians and mathematicians, and so forth. Moreover, we said that Christian thinking gradually adopted some things from the inheritance of Greek and Roman thinking to create what can only be called a Christian body of philosophy. By the same token, churchly lawyers created a body of law for the empire that drew on both old Roman law and Mosaic law (among other things). Now, by speaking of a Christian civilization in the ancient church, or in the following European Middle Ages, or in Colonial America, I do not mean, for example, that everybody obeyed the Ten Commandments. The point rather is that everybody thought that he or she was *supposed* to do so. Nor do I mean to suggest that everyone believed the gospel. The point, rather, is that the gospel was what one believed if he or she believed anything at all.

We may describe the civilization created by Christianity's interaction with the fragments of Greek and Roman civilization as a marriage. The metaphor is not only apt; it leads to another metaphor as well. If Christendom was a marriage between the gospel and Greco-Roman civilization, then we may regard Modernity as a long, drawn-out divorce. Now divorce does not leave the partners of a marriage unchanged. So we have to ask, what happens to a civilization when it abandons the very faith that founded it, when it stops believing the claims that shape and move its law and its morals and its art and its thinking? What happens when a culture stops believing the only thing it can believe as the particular culture that it is?

One possibility surely is that it will try to survive believing in nothing. Let us call this conviction that there is nothing to believe in "nihilism." The greatest exponent of nihilism was doubtless Friedrich Nietzsche. But instead of quoting Nietzsche, which I love to do, let me instead quote a remarkable passage from an earlier and, in his day, an extraordinarily popular nihilist. I am thinking of Jean Paul. The passage is often cited as "Words of the dead Christ spoken from the Universe." The narrator dreams and finds himself in a deserted church. The tombs in the church open and the shades of the dead emerge, and then "a high noble figure marked by ineradicable suffering came down from on high to the altar and all the dead cried, 'Christ, is there no God?' Christ answered, 'There is none.' Christ continued, 'I travelled through the worlds, I ascended into the stars and flew with the Milky Way through the wastes of heaven, but there is no God. I descended as far as being casts a shadow, and I cried, 'Father, where are you?' but I heard only the eternal storm that is guided and ordered by no one. And when I looked to the infinite world for a divine eye, the world stared back from an empty eye socket. Eternity rested on chaos and gnawed at it and regurgitated it and chewed on itself.'"

You could not ask for a better description of a world in which there is nothing to believe. The question it poses is this: supposing that the divorce between the gospel and Constantinian marriage has left the culture under the permanent threat of nihilism;

what challenge does that pose to the church and its theology? Why pay attention to late modern nihilism? First, because it is our world. Now since this is an introduction to Christian theology, the "we" in question is those doing Christian theology (even if they are only engaged in a classroom experiment). And since the Christian church is, as we have said, the bearer of a message, then the message must be told to *someone*. But to whom? Well, in our present situation it must be told to the denizens of the modern West who live under the threat of nihilism. So we must ask, might it be that the church and its theology, along and with everything else we have been talking about in these lectures, are in fact a pile of dead, dry bones?

Let me proceed by elaborating some of the specific challenges that nihilism poses to the church and its message. First this. The church had come, after all those centuries of the Constantinian Settlement, to depend on the general culture for the plausibility of its teachings and practices. The central message of the church, "Jesus of Nazareth has been raised from the dead," is not immediately plausible. What makes it plausible? The church had depended on the general structure of the culture to make the church's message seem plausible. For if Christianity had shaped what people learned in their homes and in school, in the literature they read and in what they saw when they went to the theater, a basis had been laid for at least understanding and perhaps for trusting the church's discourse and practice. Modernism has brought this happy marriage to an end.

But it is not just that the church and theology are in Modernity bereft of the culture's support. To continue the metaphor of marriage and divorce for a moment, separated ex-lovers often turn on each other. A messy divorce is much more common than a so-called civilized one. The church exists as the bearer of what is supposed to be good news to whatever chunk of the world it confronts at the moment, including that post-Christian Western world. The West's post-Christian culture has definitely and increasingly turned against the church and the church's theology. And, again, we must at least abstractly say that the challenge may be right. The church and its theology may indeed be a pile of dead bones which it would be best to get rid of.

This hostile challenge would be best described, I think, as a metaphysical challenge. We have used that word "metaphysics" before, but let me remind you of something that I have been insisting in these lectures: when we begin doing metaphysics—that is, when we begin asking questions like "what is it 'to be'?"—we are not just playing empty word games. The questions we ask and the answers we give both express and shape the way we perceive and act in the world. The metaphysical challenge that Modernity has posed to the church and its message has proceeded on two lines.

First, it says that there are no general truths at all. There is not any such thing as a proposition that is true for everybody all of the time. Indeed, there are only disguised agendas. So, if you hear me say, "Christ is risen!" and if you are a true late modern or post-modern individual, you will instantly ask yourself, "What is Jenson trying to sell? What is he up to? What is his interest in persuading me that Jesus was crucified, died, and buried, but nevertheless lives again? What is his agenda?" Often, the same or nearly the same point is made about narratives. We are told that there can be no true or honest meta-narratives—that is to say, no stories about how things generally are. Since, then, Christian theology does pretend to tell such a story—since it does tell about a creator of all things and of what the world is like on account of being created, and about a savior of all persons—just for that reason it is regarded by many to be not merely empty but sinister.

The great prophet of such nihilism was Friedrich Nietzsche. But next in line is the greatest and most evil philosopher of the twentieth century—Martin Heidegger. He defined authentic existence "as being toward death" and, when in a little book entitled *Introduction to Metaphysics*, he posed the question, "Why is there anything at all? Why not just nothing?" the answer he gave was, "So that there should be someone there to ask, 'Why is there anything at all? Why is there not just nothing?'" Then, at the end of the last century we had Jacques Derrida. He asked, "What makes language work?" His answer was, roughly, that it is the interior or syntactic relationships among the words within a language that make that language work. His answer was not novel. The conclusion he drew from it, however, was: Derrida said that one can never refer to what is real. If I say cow and you ask what a cow is, how do I answer? I give more language. Derrida's point was that the attachment of what we say to reality is always, as he put it, "deferred." You never actually get to the attachment. You are just going round and round and round within whatever language you are speaking.

There are two lines along which nihilism attacks the church's faith and its theology metaphysically. We have just discussed the first. The second stems from the fact that the old conversation between the gospel and the Greeks included large areas of agreement. God is rational. Everybody agreed, pagans and Christians alike. The goal of human existence is the knowledge of God. Everybody agreed with that, except the Epicureans. The world makes rough sense and the rationality discernible in the world is a reflection of God's rationality, and part of how we can

come to know God is by contemplating the rationality revealed
in the world. Morally, murder is a bad thing, parents should be
honored, death is not good, and so on. By and large such things
were uncontested.

Now, how to account for such shared beliefs between, on the
one hand, Judaism and Christianity and, on the other hand, persons who knew nothing of God's act in Israel or in Jesus Christ?
Through the Middle Ages, the notion of human nature solidified as
an explanation. Since we are all creatures of the God of Israel and
the God of Jesus Christ, whether we know it or not, it is only *natural*
to us not to be wholly ignorant of God and our relationship to him.
Thus, when such persons find surprising truths in Plato or Aristotle,
that is explicable by the fact that it is simply natural to know those
things. And then the *specifics* of Jewish or Christian faith are
sought to be *super*naturally revealed. Within the Constantinian
marriage, these two kinds of theology, natural and supernatural,
worked well together. But when Christian civilization's synthesis
came apart, natural theology and revealed theology tended to split;
one went with the secular culture and the other with the church.
And then the Enlighteners pointed out that Christian theology
itself had said that natural theology is the knowledge of God that
is natural to humans. So why should we need more? Why not just
get on with natural theology alone? And then if there are points
of tension between, let us say Plato's understanding of eternity
as the sheer absence of time and the way the Bible talks of God's
historical actions, must not the more natural theology trump in
such cases? Indeed, is not much of the allegedly supernatural theology in fact simply unnatural theology? Are not the metaphysics
of Plato or Aristotle and their successors in slightly modified ver-
sions the real framework, the natural way of regarding God and his

relationship to us, within which we have to live? Much theology of the eighteenth and nineteenth centuries accepted this order of priority: when natural theology and the allegedly supernatural theology peculiar to Christianity clash, it was natural theology that had the final say. Much of the modern history of religion in the West has been a series of desperate attempts by Christians to appease the allegedly universal rationality that was thought to be at home outside the church.

Another challenge to the church and its message is the "historical-critical method" in the interpretation of the Scriptures. A method, of course, is a self-conscious way of going about doing something. The scientific method includes at a crucial point two instructions: ignore teleology—do not ask what a thing is for; and be suspicious of how things look to begin with. That is a method; that is a self-conscious way—I have to say "self-conscious" because it is not a method until somebody has reflected on it—of going about getting something done. The historical-critical method is, then, a way of interpreting old texts—that is, texts that are far enough removed from us in time that they constitute history for us—like the Bible, or for that matter the Greek historians, or the Bhagavad Gita, or the Book of Mormon. This method became self-conscious early in Modernity and has established itself as Christianity's typical way of reading not only the Bible but the whole corpus of history and literature that had been bequeathed to us from the past. Now, when reading, say, the Gospels or *Plutarch's Lives*, our reading is *critical* if it asks the question made dominant by the dominance of the physical sciences: "That is what things look like, but are they really as they appear?" Applied to texts like a story in one of the Gospels about Jesus, the critical question has to be, "This is what according to this text Jesus is supposed to have said or done, but is that really how it went down?" Or a passage in one of Paul's letters about the Torah, "Paul thinks that the Torah works this way, but did he have it right? Would the other Rabbis of his time have agreed with him in his understanding of the Torah?"

That is the sense in which the historical-critical method is *critical*. It is *historical* in a twofold sense of the word. The first is a rather innocuous sense that if a text mentions something that is supposed to have happened, the relevant kind of critique is, "Did it really happen that way?" The critique here is an attempt to reconstruct the real history. Now, there are all kinds of pre-judgments capsulized in that word "real," but let us ignore that just for the moment. The important point is that historical-critical investigation—let us say, then, of Jesus's life—gets to be the attempt to reconstruct the life of Jesus as it *really* went down as opposed to the way the text suggests it went down. So that is the one way in which critical exegesis of texts is historical-critical, not just critical but historical-critical. Now, there is no intrinsic reason that such interpretation of the Scriptures should be a problem either for Christian or Jewish theology. The second sense in which the historical-critical method is historical, on the other hand, poses more of a problem: it insists that what a text *really* is is what it would have meant to the person who wrote the text and the persons for whom the text was originally written. What a text really says is what it would have said in its own historical context that is presumed to be different from ours. Consider, for example, the letter that Paul wrote toward the end of his career to the church in Rome that he planned to visit. It is obvious that first-century Rome was a very different spiritual and intellectual environment from Princeton. For us twenty-first-century Princetonians to understand this letter we are going to want to know something about Rome at that time. And more precisely we want to know about the ways in which its inhabitants may have thought differently about things than we do. Again, there is a perfectly harmless way of carrying on in this manner, and to some extent scholars have always asked that sort of question.

But Modernity has practiced historical-critical interpretation of old documents with unprecedented zeal. From the beginning of Modernity's use of the historical-critical method, it has wielded it with a very decided angst. And if we harp on long enough about the differences of the church in Rome to which Paul wrote and the church we now inhabit (if we inhabit one), in such a case why worry about what Paul wrote to the church in Rome? Now, I think there is a cure for that, but it is an ecclesiological one. I will come to that later on.

The question for us now is whether and how the church can respond to the challenges posed to its message by the advent of Modernity. Christian theology and the practices of the church must relearn how to display the church's or the faith's own interior plausibility—not drawing on anything outside of itself—as was done in the centuries before Constantine. Now, it may be that we cannot do that. That is to say, the bones may be bones and will stay that way; that is an abstract possibility. Within theology as such, however, the nineteenth and twentieth centuries produced a succession of great thinkers who attempted to do just that. Undoubtedly in my judgment the greatest is the Swiss theologian Karl Barth, who taught from around 1918 when the First World War ended until the Student Revolution of 1968.

Barth attempted at least to reverse the viewpoint from which the relationship of the church and culture is seen. In Modernity, everybody (including believers) has tended to suppose that the gospel and its theology have to establish their plausibility by securing a place within the broader culture. Barth turned this on its head. As a young preacher, he found himself stuck in an industrial parish that was being destroyed by laissez-faire capitalists. This made him, among other things, a socialist—but the important thing is that he had to preach out of texts from the Bible. (Like many students of theology, it had not really occurred to him that that is what a pastor must do.) So, he began to read the Bible. What he found it in was shocking. He discovered that it contains a whole world that he was not used to inhabiting. And he found that this strange new world is an all-encompassing world. National ideologies and secular historiographies? Barth said that they have to establish and justify their place within the world of the Bible, not the other way around. The question is not how we can justify Christian propositions a la Aristotle. The question, Barth said, is whether and how we can justify Aristotelian propositions a la the Bible. Now, is Barth right? I think he is, but I may be prejudiced because he was my teacher.

Let me go back and repeat myself. The inheritance within what I call the marriage between the theology of the pre-Christian Greek thinkers and the Scriptures, from the Plato, Aristotle, and the Plotinus side understands eternity as the contradiction of time. God is timeless and indeed is divine precisely by his immunity to what goes on in time. It is obvious that marrying this view to what the Bible says about God is going to be very difficult, but for centuries it worked. One way to describe the Enlightenment is to say that the marriage is dissolved—in other words, the challenge of Modernity is what I called the divorce process of this marriage. So the Enlightenment vision of God and its general metaphysics is in effect a simplified version of the pre-Christian Greek metaphysics. And the dissolution of the marriage has made plain how inhospitable it is with the story the Bible has to tell about God.

In my judgment, theology responds best by trusting in the gospel's own interior rationality, and then building its own metaphysics, its own vision of reality. This endeavor has been going on for some time actually. One point guard in the endeavor might be Wolfhart Pannenberg, who has elaborated an entire system of metaphysics (and indeed an entire philosophy of science to go with it) on the principle that traditional metaphysics draws its vision of what is from what has been, whereas a distinctively Christian metaphysics must draw its vision from what *will* be. Indeed, that is what we have been doing all along here in these lectures. We have taken the claims of Christian doctrine with absolute seriousness: that the creator of all things is triune, so that his life has a specific structure from which the structure of everything else follows, and that one of the Trinity, one of the three, is the resurrected Jewish Messiah, Jesus.

COMPREHENSIVE BIBLIOGRAPHY
OF WORKS BY ROBERT JENSON

*Robert Jenson is the author or co-author of all the works
listed in the bibliography*

"1982." *Dialog* 21.4 (Autumn 1982): 244–45.

"About Dialog, and the Church, and Some Bits of the Theological Biography of Robert W. Jenson." *Dialog* 11.4 (Autumn 1969): 38–42.

"Afterword." In *Trinitarian Soundings in Systematic Theology*, ed. Paul Louis Metzger. London: T&T Clark, 2006, 217–20.

Alpha and Omega: A Study in the Theology of Karl Barth. New York: Thomas Nelson, 1963. Reprint: Eugene, OR: Wipf and Stock, 2002.

"Always to Care, Never to Kill: A Declaration on Euthanasia" (with others). *First Things* 20 (February 1992): 45–47.

"The America of the Inaugural." *Dialog* 8.2 (Spring 1969): 84–85.

"The American People." *First Things* 92 (April 1999): 12–13.

America's Theologian: A Recommendation of Jonathan Edwards. New York: Oxford University Press, 1988.

"Anima Ecclesiastica." In *God and Human Dignity*, ed. R. Kendall Soulen and Linda Woodhead. Grand Rapids, MI: Eerdmans, 2006, 57–71.

"Apostolicity in the Gospel." *Lutheran-Episcopal Dialogue: A Progress Report*, ed. Robert Jenson et al. New York: Maxi Books, 1972, 49–61.

"Appeal to the Person of the Future." In *The Futurist Option*, by Carl E. Braaten and Robert W. Jenson. New York: Newman Press, 1970, 147–58.

"Aspects of a Doctrine of Creation." In *Doctrine of Creation: Essays in Dogmatics, History, and Philosophy*, ed. Colin E. Gunton. London: T&T Clark, 2004, 17–28.

"Aspekte der Christologie in einer pluralistischen Gesellschaft." In *Christsein in einer pluralistischen Gesellschaft*, ed. Hans Schulze and Hans Schwarz. Beiträge aus evangelischer Sicht 25. Hamburg: Wittig, 1971.

"An Attempt to Think about *Mary*." *Dialog* 31.4 (Autumn 1992): 259–64.

"The August 1997 Assembly of the ELCA." *Pro Ecclesia* 6.4 (Fall 1997): 389–92.

"Avery Cardinal Dulles." *Pro Ecclesia* 10.2 (Spring 2001): 133–34.

"Back to the Barricades." *Dialog* 21.2 (Spring 1982): 85–86.

"Baptism and Return to Baptism." *Lutheran Forum* 25.1 (Fall 1991): 40–43.

"Basics and Christology." In *In Search of Christian Unity: Basic Consensus/Basic Differences*, ed. Joseph A. Burgess. Minneapolis, MN: Fortress Press, 1991, 45–58.

"Beauty." *Dialog* 25.1 (Winter 1986): 250–54.

"The Bible and the Trinity." *Pro Ecclesia* 11.3 (Summer 2002): 329–39.

"The Body of God's Presence: A Trinitarian Theory." In *Creation, Christ, and Culture: Studies in Honor of T. F. Torrance*, ed. R. W. A. McKinney. Edinburgh: T&T Clark, 1976.

"A Call to Faithfulness." *Dialog* 30.2 (Spring 1991): 90–97.

Canon and Creed. Louisville, KY: Westminster John Knox, 2010.

"Can Deterrence Be Justified as a Lesser Evil: A Debate" (with Paul R. Hinlicky). *Currents in Theology and Mission* 12.5 (October 1985): 261–76.

"Can Holiness Be a Nota Ecclesiae?" *Bejdragen* 67.3 (2006): 245–52.

"Can a Text Defend Itself? An Essay *de Inspiratione Scripturae*." *Dialog* 28.4 (Autumn 1989): 251–56.

"Can We Have a Story?" *First Things* 101 (March 2000): 16–17.

"Catachesis for Our Time." In *Marks of the Body of Christ*, ed. Carl Braaten and Robert Jenson. Grand Rapids, MI: Eerdmans, 1999, 137–49.

"Catholic and Evangelical?" Review of *Systematic Theology*, vol. 3, by Wolfhart Pannenberg. *First Things* 86 (October 1998): 42–43.

"Central America." *Dialog* 22.4 (Autumn 1983): 244–45.

"Christ as Culture 1: Christ as Polity." *International Journal of Systematic Theology* 5 (November 2003): 323–29.

"Christ as Culture 2: Christ as Art." *International Journal of Systematic Theology* 6 (January 2004): 69–76.

"Christ as Culture 3: Christ as Drama." *International Journal of Systematic Theology* 6 (April 2004): 194–201.

"Christ-Dogma and Christ-Image." *Dialog* 2.2 (Spring 1963): 146–51.

"Christ in the Trinity: *Communicatio Idiomatum.*" In *The Person of Christ*, ed. Stephen Holmes and Murray Rae. London: T&T Clark, 2005, 61–69.

"Christian Civilization." In *God, Truth, and Witness: Engaging Stanley Hauerwas*, ed. L. Gregory Jones, Reinhard Hütter, and C. Rosalee Velloso Ewell. Grand Rapids, MI: Brazos, 2005, 153–63.

"The Christian Doctrine of God." In *Keeping the Faith: Essays to Mark the Centenary of Lux Mundi*, ed. Geoffrey Wainwright. London: SPCK, 1985, 25–53.

Christian Dogmatics, 2 vols., ed. Carl Braaten and Robert Jenson. Philadelphia: Fortress Press, 1984.

"Christian Initiation: Ethics and Eschatology." *Christian Initiation: Institute of Liturgical Studies Occasional Papers.* Valparaiso, IN: Institute of Liturgical Studies, 1981, 58–72.

"The Christological Objectivity of History." In *Story Lines: Chapters on Thought, Word, and Deed*, ed. Skye Fackre Gibson. Grand Rapids, MI: Eerdmans, 2002, 62–67.

"The Church as *Communio.*" In *The Catholicity of the Reformation*, ed. Carl Braaten and Robert Jenson. Grand Rapids, MI: Eerdmans, 1996.

"The Church as Communion: A Catholic-Lutheran Dialoge-Consensus-Statement Dreamed in the Night." *Pro Ecclesia* 4.1 (Winter 1995): 68–78.

"The Church and Mass Electronic Media: The Hermeneutic Problem." *Religious Education* 82.2 (Spring 1987): 270–84.

"The Church and the Sacraments." In *The Cambridge Companion to Christian Doctrine*, ed. Colin Gunton. New York: Cambridge University Press, 1997.

"The Church's Responsibility for the World." In *Two Cities of God: The Church's Responsibility for the Earthly City*, ed. Carl E. Braaten and Robert W. Jenson. Grand Rapids, MI: Eerdmans, 1997, 1–10.

120   *Bibliography*

"Comment on a Common Calling." *Pro Ecclesia* 1.1 (Fall 1992): 16–20.

"Conceptus ... de Spiritu Sancto." *Pro Ecclesia* 15.1 (Winter 2006): 100–107.

"Concerning, and Illustrating New Orders for the Eucharist." *Dialog* 10.1 (Winter 1971): 68–72.

Conversations with Poppi about God (with Lucia Solveig Gold). Grand Rapids, MI: Brazos, 2006.

"Creation as a Triune Act." *Word and World* 2.1 (Winter 1982): 34–42.

"Creator and Creature." *International Journal of Systematic Theology* 4 (July 2002): 216–21.

"The Creed." *Lutheran Forum* 24.1 (Fall 1990): 34–36.

"The D in Chicago." *Dialog* 22.2 (Spring 1983): 138–39.

"A Dead Issue Revisited." *Lutheran Quarterly* 14.1 (Fall 1962): 53–56.

"Death in Vitro." *Pro Ecclesia* 4.1 (Winter 1995): 13–15.

"The Decalogue." *Lutheran Forum* 23.4 (November 1989): 12–14.

"A Decision Tree of Colin Gunton's Thinking." *Theology of Colin Gunton*. London: T&T Clark, 2010, 8–16.

"Die Kontinuität vom Alten und Neuem Testament als Problem für Kirche und Theologie heute." *Hoffnung ohne Illusion*, ed. H. Zeddies. Berlin [East]: Evangelische Verlagsanstalt, 1970, 88–103.

"Does God Have Time? The Doctrine of the Trinity and the Concept of Time in the Physical Sciences." *CTNS Bulletin: The Center for Theology and the Natural Sciences* 11.1 (Winter 1991): 1–6.

"The Doxological Concept of History in the Theology of Peter Brunner." In *Zur Auferbauung Des Liebes Christi: Festgabe für Professor D. Peter Brunner*, ed. Edmund Schlink and Albrecht Peters. Kassel: Johannes Stauda-Verlag, 1965, 181–98.

"Duplication Forever." *Dialog* 20.4 (Autumn 1981): 266–67.

"Election and Culture: From Babylon to Jerusalem." In *Public Theology in Cultural Engagement*, ed. Stephen R. Holmes. Milton Keynes, UK: Paternoster, 2008, 48–61.

"El Salvador." *Dialog* 20.3 (Summer 1981): 184–85.

"The Elusive Bottom Lines." *Dialog* 29.2 (Spring 1990): 111–18.

"The End Is Music." In *Edwards in Our Time: Jonathan Edwards and the Shaping of American Religion*, ed. Sang Hyun Lee and Allen C. Guelzo. Grand Rapids, MI: Eerdmans, 1999, 161–71.

"Epiphany." *Theology Today* 60.4 (January 2004): 559.

"Eschatological Politics and Political Eschatology." *Dialog* 8.4 (Autumn 1969): 272–78.

"Eschatological Politics and Political Eschatology." In *The Futurist Option*, by Carl E. Braaten and Robert W. Jenson. New York: Newman Press, 1970, 93–106.

Essays in Theology of Culture. Grand Rapids, MI: Eerdmans, 1995.

"Eucharist: Its Relative Necessity, Specific Warrant, and Traditional Order." *Dialog* 14.2 (Spring 1975): 122–33.

"Evil as Person." *Lutheran Theological Seminary Bulletin* 69.1 (Winter 1980): 33–40.

"The Eye, the Ear, and Lutheranism." *Dialog* 29.3 (Summer 1990): 174–77.

Ezekiel. Grand Rapids, MI: Brazos, 2009.

"Faithfulness." *Dialog* 14.1 (Winter 1975): 38–41.

"The Father, he . . ." In *Speaking the Christian God: The Holy Trinity and the Challenge of Feminism*, ed. Alvin F. Kimel. Grand Rapids, MI: Eerdmans, 1992, 95–109.

"Film, Preaching, and Meaning." In *Celluloid and Symbols*, ed. John Charles Cooper and Carl Skrade. Philadelphia, PA: Fortress Press, 1970, 41–49.

"For Us . . . He Was Made Man." In *Nicene Christianity: The Future for a New Ecumenism*, ed. Christopher R. Seitz. Grand Rapids, MI: Brazos, 2001, 75–85.

"The Future of the Papacy: A Symposium." *First Things* 111 (March 2001): 28–36.

"The Futurist Option of Speaking of God." *Lutheran Quarterly* 21.1 (February 1969): 17–25.

God after God. The God of the Past and the God of the Future, Seen in the Work of Karl Barth. New York: Bobbs-Merrill, 1969.

"'Gott' als Antwort." *Evangelische Theologie* 26.7 (July 1966): 368–78.

"Gott als Antwort." In *Philosophische Theologie im Schatten des Nihilismus*, ed. Jörg Salaguarda. Berlin: De Gruyter, 1971, 146–59.

"The God Question." *Lutheran Forum* 26.4 (November 1992): 46–50.

"God, Space and Architecture." In *The Futurist Option*, by Carl E. Braaten and Robert W. Jenson. New York: Newman Press, 1970, 165–73.

"The God-Wars." In *Either/Or: The Gospel of Neopaganism*, ed. Carl E. Braaten and Robert W. Jenson. Grand Rapids, MI: Eerdmans, 1995, 23–36.

"The Great Transformation." In *Last Things: Biblical and Theological Perspectives on Eschatology*, ed. Carl E. Braaten and Robert W. Jenson. Grand Rapids, MI: Eerdmans, 2002, 33–42.

"Gregory of Nyssa, the Life of Moses." *Theology Today* 62.4 (January 2006): 533–37.

"Gunton, Colin E., 1941–2003." *Theology Today* 61.1 (April 2004): 85.

"The Hauerwas Project." *Modern Theology* 8.3 (July 1992): 285–95.

"Hermeneutical Apology for Systematics." *Dialog* 4.4 (Autumn 1965): 268–74.

"Hermeneutics and the Life of the Church." In *Reclaiming the Bible for the Church*, ed. Carl Braaten and Robert Jenson. Grand Rapids: Eerdmans, 1995, 89–105.

"The Hidden and Triune God." *International Journal of Systematic Theology* 2.1 (March 2000): 5–12.

"The Homosexual Movement." *First Things* 41 (March 1994): 15–21.

"How Long?" *Dialog* 29.1 (Winter 1990): 4–5.

"How the World Lost Its Story." *First Things* 36.1 (October 1993): 19–24.

"Identity, Jesus, and Exegesis." *Seeking the Identity of Jesus*, ed. Beverly Roberts Gaventa and Richard B. Hays. Grand Rapids, MI: Eerdmans, 2008, 43–59.

"The Inclusive Lectionary." *Dialog* 23.1 (Winter 1984): 4–6.

"An Inclusive St. Patrick's Day in New York." *Pro Ecclesia* 2.2 (Spring 1993): 137–38.

"The Inhuman Use of Human Beings." *First Things* 49 (January 1995): 17–21.

"*Ipse Pater Non Est Impassibilis*." In *Divine Impassibility and the Mystery of Human Suffering*, ed. James F. Keating and Thomas Joseph White. Grand Rapids, MI: Eerdmans, 2009, 117–26.

"Is Patriotism a Virtue?" In *God and Country?* ed. Michael G. Long and Tracy Wenger Sadd. New York: Macmillan, 2007, 147–53.

"A Jeremiad from the New Editor." *Dialog* 14.1 (Winter 1975): 4–6.

"Jesus, Father, Spirit: The Logic of the Doctrine of the Trinity." *Dialog* 26.4 (Autumn1987): 245–49.

"Jesus in the Trinity." *Pro Ecclesia* 8.3 (Summer 1999): 308–18.

"Jesus in the Trinity: Wolfhart Pannenberg's Christology and Doctrine of the Trinity." In *Theology of Wolfhart Pannenberg: Twelve American Critiques with an Autobiographical Essay and Response*, ed. Carl E. Braaten and Phillip Clayton. Minneapolis, MN: 1988, 188–206.

"Joining the Eternal Conversation: John's Prologue and the Language of Worship." *Touchstone* 14.9 (November 2001): 32–37.

"Justification as a Triune Event." *Modern Theology* 11 (October 1995): 421–27.

"Karl Barth." In *The Modern Theologians*, 3rd ed., ed. David Ford and Rachel Muers. Great Theologians Series. Oxford: Oxford University Press, 2005, 147–53.

The Knowledge of Things Hoped For: The Sense of Theological Discourse. Oxford: Oxford University Press, 1969.

"Kristendommen og religionerne," trans. Karsten Farup Hansen and Lars Sandbeck. *Dansk teologisk tidsskrift* 72.4 (2009): 241–49.

"Language and Time." *Response* 8 (1966): 75–80.

A Large Catechism. Delhi, NY: ALPB, 1991.

"The LCA, Centralization, Gospel Authority, and the Lutheran Clergy Association." *Dialog* 11.2 (Spring 1972): 89.

"A Lenten Sermon." *Dialog* 21.3 (Summer 1982): 229–30.

"A Lesson to Us All." *Pro Ecclesia* 3.2 (Spring 1994): 133–35.

"The Leuenberg Agreement in the North American Context." In *The Leuenberg Agreement and Lutheran-Reformed Relationships*, ed.

William G. Rusch and Daniel F. Martensen. Minneapolis, MN: Fortress Press, 1989, 97–106.

"Liberating Truth and Liberal Education." *Lutheran Quarterly* 13.3 (August 1961): 211–17.

"Liturgy of the Spirit." *Lutheran Quarterly* 26.2 (May 1974): 189–203.

"The Logos Ensarkos and Reason" (with Colin E. Gunton). In *Reason and the Reasons of Faith*, ed. Paul J. Griffiths and Reinhard Hütter. Theology for the Twenty-First Century. London: T&T Clark, 2005, 78–85.

"The Lord's Supper." *Lutheran Forum* 25.2 (May 1991): 41–44.

"Lutheran Conditions for Communion in Holy Things." *Concordia Theologial Monthly* 43.10 (November 1972): 687–92.

"A Lutheran among Friendly Pentecostals." *Journal of Pentecostal Theology* 20.1 (2011): 48–53.

"Lutheran Seminary Education in the Near Future." *Trinity Seminary Review* 6 (1984): 12–15.

"LXX." *Dialog* 21.4 (Autumn 1982): 246.

"The LXX in Chicago." *Dialog* 22.2 (Spring 1983): 137.

"Male and Female He Created Them." In *I Am the Lord Your God: Christian Reflections on the Ten Commandments*, ed. Carl Braaten and Christopher Seitz. Grand Rapids, MI: Eerdmans, 2005.

"The Managers at Baltimore." *Dialog* 13.4 (Autumn 1974): 249–50.

"The Mandate and Promise of Baptism." *Interpretation* 30.3 (July 1976): 271–87.

"Marriage and Ministry." *Lutheran Forum* 31.4 (Winter 1997): 20–22.

"Missouri and the Existential Fear of Change." *Dialog* 14.4 (Autumn 1975): 247–50.

"Modernity's Undermining of Its Own Foundations." *Trinity Seminary Review* 18.1 (Summer 1996): 5–12.

"Modest Proposals: 2." *Dialog* 23.4 (Autumn 1984): 286–87.

"Moses and the Mountain of Knowledge." In *Crisis, Call, and Leadership in the Abrahamic Traditions*. New York: Palgrave Macmillan, 2009, 223–30.

"Mr. Edwards' Affections." *Dialog* 24.3 (Summer 1985): 169–75.

"Neuhaus, Richard John, 1936–2009." *Pro Ecclesia* 18.3 (Summer 2009): 239–40.

"Now What." *Dialog* 26.1 (Winter 1987): 6.

"Odysseus, Ulysses, and the Wanderer." *Dialog* 3.3 (Summer 1964): 179–84.

"On Abortion: Sorting Out the Questions—A Lutheran Contribution to the Public Policy Debate." *Lutheran Forum* 17.1 (Lent 1983): 9–12.

"On the Ascension." In *Loving God with Our Minds: The Pastor as Theologian*, ed. Michael Welker and Cynthia Jarvis. Grand Rapids, MI: Eerdmans, 2004, 331–40.

"On the Authorities of Scripture." In *Engaging Biblical Authority: Perspectives on the Bible as Scripture*, ed. William P. Brown. Louisville, KY: Westminster John Knox Press, 2007.

"On Becoming a Man." In *The Futurist Option*, by Carl E. Braaten and Robert W. Jenson. New York: Newman, 1970, 107–20.

"Once More into the Breach: The True Historical Jesus." In *Theology in the Service of the Church: Essays in Honor of Thomas W. Gillespie*, ed. Wallace M. Alston Jr. Grand Rapids, MI: Eerdmans, 2000, 120–27.

"Once More the Jesus of History and the Christ of Faith." *Dialog* 11.2 (Spring 1972): 118–24.

"Once More the *Logos Asarkos*." *International Journal of Systematic Theology* 13.2 (April 2011): 130–33.

"On Communicidal Hatters." *Dialog* 22.3 (Summer 1983): 166–67.

"On the Decadence of American Politics." *Dialog* 24.1 (Winter 1985): 6–7.

"On the Doctrine of Atonement." *Princeton Seminary Bulletin* 27.2 (2006): 100–108.

"On the ELCA's Ecumenical Choices." *Dialog* 35.3 (Summer 1996): 222–23.

"'One New, Inclusive, and Lutheran Church.'" *Dialog* 25.1 (Winter 1986): 2–3.

"On Hegemonic Discourse." *First Things* 45 (August–September 1994): 13–15.

"On Infant Baptism." *Dialog* 8.3 (Summer 1969): 214–17.

"On Infant Communion Again." *Lutheran Forum* 30.4 (Winter 1996): 18.

"On the 'Joint Declaration of the Lutheran World Federation and the Roman Catholic Church on the Doctrine of Justification.'" *Pro Ecclesia* 5.2 (Spring 1996): 137–41.

"On Lutheranism and Cozy Ecumenism." *Dialog* 28.4 (Autumn 1989): 242–43.

"On the Problem(s) of Scriptural Authority." *Interpretation* 31 (July 1977): 237–50.

"On Seminaries in Long Retrospect." *Dialog* 28.2 (Spring 1989): 87–91.

On Thinking the Human: Resolutions of Difficult Notions. Grand Rapids, MI: Eerdmans, 2003.

"On Truth and God. 1, *Ipsa Veritas* and Late Modernity." *Pro Ecclesia* 20.4 (Fall 2011): 384–88.

"On Truth and God, 2, the Triunity of Truth." *Pro Ecclesia* 21.1 (2012): 51–55.

"Orpheus, the Buttonmaker, and Real Community." *Dialog* 10.1 (Winter 1971): 32–38.

"On the Vatican's 'Official Response' to the Joint Declaration on Justification." *Pro Ecclesia* 7.4 (Fall 1998): 401–4.

"An Orthodox/Reformation Consensus." *Pro Ecclesia* 2.4 (Fall 1993): 400–403."Parting Ways? Review of *Systematic Theology*, vol. 2, by Wolfhart Pannenberg." *First Things* 53 (May 1995): 60–62.

"The Pastor Roth Case." *Dialog* 24.2 (Spring 1985): 85–86.

"Pittsburgh Again." *Dialog* 24.3 (Summer 1985): 165.

"The Plot Not to Kidnap Kissinger." *Dialog* 11.2 (Spring 1972): 88–89.

"The Praying Animal." *Zygon* 18.3 (September 1983): 311–25.

"The Preacher, the Text and Certain Dogmas." *Dialog* 21.2 (Spring 1982): 107–13.

"Preus' Statement: Its Heresy and Foolishness." *Dialog* 11.3 (Summer 1972): 164–65.

"Principles of Atheological Education." *Dialog* 25.1 (Winter 1986): 59–60.

"Proclamation without Metaphysics." *Dialog* 1.4 (Autumn 1962): 22–29.

"A 'Protestant Constructive Response' to Christian Unbelief." In *American Apostasy: The Triumph of 'Other' Gospels*, ed. Richard John Neuhaus. Grand Rapids, MI: Eerdmans, 1989, 56–74.

"Psalm 32." *Interpretation* 33.2 (April 1979): 172–76.

"Rechtfertigung als dreieiniges Ereignis." *Rechtfertigung und Erfahrung: Fur Gerhard Sauter zum 60 Geburtstag*, ed. Gerhard Sauter and Michael Beintker. Gütersloh, Germany: Kaiser, 1995, 104–12.

"Rechtfertigung und Ekklesiologie." *Kerygma und Dogma* 42.3 (July–September 1996): 202–17.

"Reflections on a Burst of Patriotism(?)." *Dialog* 30.2 (Spring 1991): 88–89.

A Religion against Itself. Richmond: John Knox Press, 1967.

"Religious Pluralism, Christology and Barth." *Dialog* 20 (Winter 1982): 31–38.

"The Religious Power of Scripture." *Scottish Journal of Theology* 1 (1999): 89–105.

"Reply to Peters on 'Sacrifice.'" *Dialog* 24.4 (Autumn 1985): 299–300.

"Re-review: Karl Barth's The Word of God and the Word of Man." *Modern Churchman* 25.4 (1983): 51–54.

"Response." *Dialog* 7.3 (Summer 1968): 229–30.

"Response." *Union Seminary Quarterly Review* 28.1 (Fall 1972): 31–34.

"Response to Mark Seifrid, Paul Metzger, and Carl Trueman on Finnish Luther Research." *Westminster Theological Journal* 62.2 (Fall 2003): 245–50.

"Response to Philadelphia." *Dialog* 31.2 (Spring 1992): 155–56.

Response to "Review of *Religion Against Itself*, by Robert Jenson." *Dialog* 7.3 (Summer 1968): 229–30.

"Response to Robert Davis Hughes III." *Sewanee Theological Review* 45.1 (Christmas 2001): 72–74.

"Response to Timo Tavast." *Pro Ecclesia* 19.4 (Fall 2010): 369–70.

"Response to Watson and Hunsinger." *Scottish Journal of Theology* 55.2 (2002): 225–28.

"The Return to Baptism." In *Encounters with Luther,* vol. 2, ed. Eric W. Gritsch. Gettysburg, PA: Lutheran Theological Seminary, 1982, 217–25.

"Reversals: How My Mind Has Changed." *Christian Century* 127.8 (April 2010): 30–33.

"Review Essay: David Bentley Hart, *The Beauty of the Infinite: The Aesthetics of Christian Truth.*" *Pro Ecclesia* 14.2 (Spring 2005), 235–37.

Review of *A Christian Critique of American Culture: An Essay in Practical Theology,* by Julian Norris Hartt. *Dialog* 7.4 (Autumn 1968): 309.

Review of *After Christendom: How the Church Is to Behave if Freedom, Justice, and a Christian Nation Are Bad Ideas,* by Stanley Hauerwas. *First Things* 25 (August–September 1992): 49–51.

Review of *Anselm: Fides Quaerens Intellectum,* by Karl Barth. *Dialog* 1.1 (Winter 1962): 77–78.

Review of *Ascension and Ecclesia: On the Significance of the Ascension for Ecclesiology and Christian Cosmology,* by Douglas Farrow. *Princeton Seminary Bulletin* 22.1 (2001): 101–2.

Review of *Barth's Moral Theology: Human Action in Barth's Thought,* by John Webster. *International Journal of Systematic Theology* 2.1 (March 2000), 119–21.

Review of *Celebration of Awareness: A Call for Institutional Revolution,* by Ivan Ilich. *Dialog* 10.3 (Summer 1971): 224–25.

Review of *Christ and Counter-Christ: Apocalyptic Themes in Theology and Culture,* by Carl E. Braaten. *Dialog* 11.4 (Autumn 1972): 310–12.

Review of *Christ, History and Apocalyptic: The Politics of Christian Mission,* by Nathan R. Kerr. *Pro Ecclesia* 20.3 (Summer 2011): 310–12.

Review of *Christ in a Pluralistic Age,* by John J. Cobb Jr. *Interpretation* 31.3 (July 1977): 307–11.

Review of *Christian Faith and History: A Critical Comparison of Ernst Troeltsch and Karl Barth,* by Thomas W. Ogletree. *Lutheran World* 13.3 (1966): 343.

Review of *Ethics with Barth: God, Metaphysics, and Morals,* by Matthew F. Rose. *First Things* 212 (April 2011): 64–65.

Review of *Fabric of Paul Tillich's Theology,* by David H. Kelsey. *Journal of Theological Studies* (New Series) 19.2 (October 1968): 691–93.

Review of *Jonathan Edwards: A New Biography,* by Iain H. Murray. *Christian Century* 106.21 (July 5–12 1989): 662.

Review of *Jonathan Edwards: The Valley and Nature: An Interpretive Essay*, by Clyde A. Holbrook. *Christian Century* 106.21 (July 2–12, 1989): 662.

Review of *Justification: The Doctrine of Karl Barth and a Catholic Reflection*, by Hans Küng. *Dialog* 5.3 (Summer 1966): 231–32.

Review of *Justification: The Heart of the Christian Faith*, by Eberhard Jüngel. *Princeton Seminary Bulletin* 23 (2002): 243–45.

Review of *Kerygma or Gospel Tradition—Which Came First?* by Robert A. Bartels. *Dialog* 1.2 (Spring 1962): 71.

Review of *Language, Hermeneutic, and Word of God*, by Robert W. Funk. *Lutheran World* 16.2 (1969): 197–98.

Review of *Manhood and Christ: A Study in the Christology of Theodore of Mopsuestia*, by Richard A. Norris. *Dialog* 3.4 (Autumn 1964): 306–8.

Review of *On Christian Theology,* by Rowan Williams. *Pro Ecclesia* 9.3 (2002): 367–69.

Review of *On Theology*, by Schubert M. Ogden. *Thomist* 51.3 (July 1987): 521–24.

Review of *Pro ecclesia: die dogmatische Theologie Peter Brunners*, by Tobias Eissler. *Theologische Literaturzeitung* 129 (January 2004), 60–61.

Review of *Radical Theology and the Death of God*, by Thomas J. J. Altizer. *Lutheran World* 14.1 (1967): 107–11.

Review of *Revelation and Theology: The Gospel as Narrated Promise*, by Ronald F. Thiemann. *Dialog* 26.1 (Winter 1987): 64–65.

Review of *Risk and Rhetoric in Religion: Whitehead's Theory of Language and the Discourse of Faith*, by Lyman T. Lundeen. *Lutheran Quarterly* 24.4 (1972): 410–12.

Review of *Suspicion and Faith: The Religious Uses of Modern Atheism*, by Merold Westphal. *First Things* 42 (April 1994): 46–48.

Review of *That They May All Be One: The Call To Unity Today*, by Walter Cardinal Kasper. *Theological Studies* 67.3 (2006): 709–10.

Review of *The Christian God*, by Richard Swinburne. *First Things* 55 (August–September 1995): 63.

Review of *The Doctrine of the Trinity: God's Being Is in Becoming*, by Eberhard Jüngel." *Interpretation* 32.1 (January 1978): 104–5.

Review of *The Drama and the Symbols: A Book on Images of God and the Problems They Raise*, by Gustav Aulén. *Theology Today* 28.3 (October 1971): 373–75.

Review of *The Essence of Christianity*, by Bruno Forte. *Theology Today* 61.2 (July 2004): 240–41.

Review of *The Fire Next Time*, by James Baldwin. *Dialog* 3.2 (Spring 1964): 146–47.

Review of *The Form of a Servant: A Historical Analytic of the Kenotic Motif*, by Donald G. Dawe. *Dialog* 3.4 (Autumn 1964): 306–8.

Review of *The Gospel of Christian Atheism*, by Thomas J. J. Altizer. *Lutheran World* 14.1 (1967): 107–11.

Review of *The Historian and the Believer: The Morality of Historical Knowledge and Christian Belief*, by Harvey van Austin. *Dialog* 6.4 (Autumn 1967): 302–4.

Review of *The Jews from Cyrus to Herod*, by Norman H. Snaith. *Lutheran Quarterly* 9.2 (May 1957): 191–92.

Review of *The Language of Faith: An Introduction to the Semantic Dilemma in the Early Church*, by Samuel Laeuchli. *Dialog* 3.1 (Winter 1964): 71–73.

Review of *The Ordinary Transformed: Karl Rahner and the Christian Vision of Transcendence*, by R. R. Reno. *First Things* 61 (March 1996): 49–50.

Review of *The Philosophical Theology of Jonathan Edwards*, by Sang Hyun Lee. *Christian Century* 106. 21 (July 5–12, 1989): 662.

Review of *The Reality of Christianity: A Study of Adolf von Harnack as Historian and Theologian*, by Wayne G. Glick. *Una Sancta* 25.2 (Pentecost 1968): 115–17.

Review of *The Social God and the Relational Self*, by Stanley J. Grenz. *Theologische Literaturzeitung* 129 (Fall 2004): 195.

Review of *Thomas Aquinas and Karl Barth: Sacred Doctrine and the Natural Knowledge of God*, by Eugene Rogers. *First Things* 69 (January 1997): 52–53.

Review of *The Theology of Wolfhart Pannenberg*, by E. Frank Tupper, *Review & Expositor* 71.4 (Fall 1974): 537–39.

Review of *The Trinity: An Interdisciplinary Symposium on the Trinity* ed. Stephen T. Davis, Daniel Kendall, and Gerald O'Collins. *Theology Today* 57.4 (January 2001): 580–82.

Review of *Unfinished Man and the Imagination: Toward an Ontology and a Rhetoric of Revelation*, by Ray L. Hart. *Lutheran World* 17.2 (1970): 195.

"Robert Wilken." *Pro Ecclesia* 3.4 (Fall 1994): 405–6.

"Say It Ain't So, Herb." *Dialog* 30.4 (Autumn 1991): 264.

"Scripture's Authority in the Church." In *The Art of Reading Scripture*, ed. Ellen F. Davis and Richard B. Hays. Grand Rapids, MI: Eerdmans, 2003.

"A Second Thought about Inspiration." *Pro Ecclesia* 13.4 (Fall 2004): 393–98.

"Second Thoughts about Theologies of Hope." *Evangelical Quarterly* 72 (2000): 335–46.

"A Sermon on the Festival of the Reformation." In *Encounters with Luther,* vol. 2, ed. Eric W. Gritsch. Gettysburg, PA: Lutheran Theological Seminary, 1982, 119–23.

"A Space for God." In *Mary, Mother of God*, ed. Carl E. Braaten and Robert Jenson. Grand Rapids, MI: Eerdmans, 2004, 49–57.

"Simplistic Thoughts about the Authority of Scripture." *Word & World* 1 (1992): 181–90.

"Some Contentious Aspects of Communion." *Pro Ecclesia* 2.2 (Spring 1993): 133–37.

"Some Platitudes about Prayer." *Dialog* 9.1 (Winter 1970): 60–66.

Song of Songs. Interpretation. Louisville, KY: John Knox Press, 2005.

"The 'Sorry' State of Lutherans." *Dialog* 22.4 (Autumn 1983): 280–83.

"Sovereignty in the Church." In *New Church Debate: Issues Facing American Lutheranism*, ed. Carl E. Braaten. Minneapolis, MN: Fortress, 1983, 39–53.

"So Why Did Braaten Do It?" *Dialog* 30.4 (Autumn 1991): 262–63.

"Stop the Merger." *Dialog* 25.3 (Summer 1986): 162–63.

Story and Promise: A Brief Theology of the Gospel about Jesus. Philadelphia: Fortress Press, 1973.

"The Strange New World of the Bible." In *Sharper Than a Two-Edged Sword*, 22–31. Grand Rapids, MI: Eerdmans, 2008.

Systematic Theology: The Triune God, vol. 1. New York: Oxford University Press, 1997.

Systematic Theology: The Works of God, vol. 2. New York: Oxford University Press, 1999.

"A Symposium on Ut Unum Sint" (with others). *Pro Ecclesia* 4.4 (Fall 1995): 389–95.

"Thanks to Yeago." *Dialog* 31.1 (Winter 1992): 22–23.

"A Theological Autobiography, to Date." *Dialog* 46.2 (Spring 2007): 46–54.

"Theosis." *Dialog*, 32.2 (Spring 1993): 18–112.

"Three Identities of One Action." *Scottish Journal of Theology* 28.1 (1975): 1–15.

"Toward a Christian Theology of Israel." *Pro Ecclesia* 9 (2000): 43–56.

"Toward a Christian Theory of the Public." *Dialog* 23.3 (Summer 1984): 191–97.

"Toward a Theology of Religions." *CGST Journal* 40 (January 2006): 69–81.

"Toward an Understanding of '... Is Risen.'" *Dialog* 19.1 (Winter 1980): 31–6.

"Toward Reform of the Lutheran Liturgical Tradition." In *Encounters with Luther*, vol. 2, ed. Eric W. Gritsch. Gettysburg, PA: Lutheran Theological Seminary, 1982, 42–51.

"The Trinity in the Bible." *Concordia Theological Quarterly* 68.3–4 (July–October 2004): 195–206.

"The Trinity and Church Structure." In *Shaping Our Future: Challenges for the Church in the Twenty-First Century*, ed. J. Stephen Freeman, 15–26. Cambridge, MA: Cowley, 1994.

"The Trinity in Ezekiel." *Lutheran Forum* 44.4 (Winter 2010): 8–10.

"Triplex Usus of Worldly Learning." *Lutheran Quarterly* 14.2 (May 1962): 121–25.

"The Triune God." In *Christian Dogmatics*, 2 vols., vol 1., ed. Carl E. Braaten and Robert W. Jenson. Philadelphia: Fortress Press, 1984, 79–191.

"Triune Grace." *Dialog* 41.1 (Winter 2002): 285–93.

The Triune Identity. Minneapolis, MN: Fortress Press, 1982.

Unbaptized God: The Basic Flaw in Ecumenical Theology. Minneapolis, MN: Fortress Press, 1992.

"The US Lutheran-Roman Dialogue on Justification by Faith." *Dialog* 23.2 (Spring 1984): 84–85.

"The Vatican, Father Curran, and Us." *Dialog* 26.1 (Winter 1987): 7–8.

"Versöhnung in Gott," trans. Dorothea H. Lorenz. In *Entzogenheit in Gott: Beiträge zur Rede von der Verborgenheit der Trinität*, ed. Markus Mühling and Martin Wendte. Ars Disputandi Supplement Series 2. Utrecht: Ars Disputandi, 2005, 31–38.

"Viet Nam: A Comment." *Dialog* 5.2 (Spring 1966): 84–85.

"Vietnamization Means War." *Dialog* 10.2 (Spring 1971): 90–91.

Visible Words: The Interpretation and Practice of the Christian Sacraments. Philadelphia: Fortress Press, 1978.

"What Ails Lutheranism." *Dialog* 30.1 (Winter 1991): 3–4.

"What Did Forde Mean?" *Dialog* 28.4 (Autumn 1989): 303.

"What Difference Post-Modernity Makes for the Church." *Trinity Seminary Review* 18.2 (Winter 1997): 83–92.

"What if the Document on Justification Were Adopted." *Pro Ecclesia* 6.1 (Winter 1997): 99–105.

"What if It Were True?" *Neue Zeitschrift für Systematische Theologie und Religionsphilosophie* 43 (2001): 3–16.

"What Is a Post-Christian?" In *Strange New Word of the Gospel: Re-Evangelizing in the Postmodern World*, ed. Robert W. Jenson and Carl E. Braaten. Grand Rapids, MI: Eerdmans, 2002, 21–31.

"What Is Salvation?" *Dialog* 12.3 (Summer 1973): 197–205.

"What Is the Point of Trinitarian Theology?" In *Trinitarian Theology Today*, ed. Christoph Schwöbel. Edinburgh: T&T Clark, 1995, 1–30.

"Whatever Sort of Juice Are They Stewing in, Up There in Saint Anthony Park." *Dialog* 30.2 (Spring 1991): 85–86.

"When Is a Conspiracy?" *Dialog* 10.2 (Spring 1971): 91–92.

"Wilhelm Dilthey and a Background Problem of Theology." *Lutheran Quarterly* 15.3 (August 1963): 212–22.

"With No Qualifications: The Christological Maximalism of the Christian East." *Ancient and Postmodern Christianity: Paleo-Orthodoxy in the 21st Century: Essays in Honor of Thomas C. Oden.* Downers Grove, IL: InterVarsity, 2002, 13–22.

"Worship as Drama." In *The Futurist Option*, by Carl E. Braaten and Robert W. Jenson. New York: Newman, 1970, 159–64.

"Worship as Word and Tone." In *The Futurist Option*, by Carl E. Braaten and Robert W. Jenson. New York: Newman Press, 1970, 175–83.

"You Wonder Where the Body Went." *CTNS Bulletin* 11.1 (Winter 1991): 20–24.

"You Wonder Where the Spirit Went." *Pro Ecclesia* 2 (1993): 296–304.

"The Youth and Age of Theological Journals" (with Carl E. Braaten). *Pro Ecclesia* 3.1 (Winter 1994): 22–23.

INDEX

Abelard, 85

Abram/Abraham, 14–16, 17–18, 21, 23, 31, 58, 69, 73

the Adam, 52–54, 57–59, 73

Alexander the Great, 24–25, 41

angels, 49, 60

animals, creation of, 61, 68

Anselm of Canterbury, 83–85

Apologists, 43

Apolos, 95

apostolicity of the church, 99–102

Aristotle, 41, 43, 68–69, 80, 99, 105, 110, 114

Arius and Arianism, 45–46

Assyrians, 21

Astarte, 23

Athanasius of Alexandria, *On the Incarnation*, 2, 47, 82

atonement, doctrine of, 72–73, 78–85

Augustine of Hippo, 70, 76, 94; *Confessions*, 2, 75

Aulen, Gustav, *Christus Victor*, 81

Babylonians, 11, 21–22, 23, 56

Balthasar, Hans Urs von, 115; *Mysterium Paschale*, 2, 86; *Theodramatik*, 86–87

Barabbas, 25

Barth, Karl, 70, 113–14

Bible. *See* Scriptures

biblical citations: Acts 2:36, 78; Ezekiel 37:3, 2, 11; Genesis 1, 58–60; Genesis 12:1-3, 14; John 3:16, 85; John 17, 90; Romans 6, 80

bilateral dialogues, 93

bishops, 101–2, 103–4

Bonhoeffer, Dietrich, *Letters and Papers from Prison*, 2

Bultmann, Rudolf, 9

"can these bones live?," 2, 5, 11–12, 32, 103, 113

Cappadocians, 47–48

catholicity of the church, 97–99

Christ, origins of term, 24. *See also* Jesus

Christian civilization, creation of, 104–5

Christian theology. *See* theology

the church, 4–5, 88–102; apostolicity of, 99–102; catholicity of, 97–99; death and resurrection of Jesus and, 79–80; the good life, communal definition of, 74; holiness of, 93–97; as missionary movement, 36, 40, 79; oneness of, 89–93; theology as community activity, 6–8, 88

135